YOUR GARDEN IN WAR-TIME

WYOUR GARDEN *in* AR-TIME

C.H. Middleton

Aurum

First published in this new edition
2010 by Aurum Press Ltd
7 Greenland Street
London NW1 0ND
www.aurumpress.co.uk

First published in 1941

A catalogue record for this book is available from the British Library.

ISBN 978 1 84513 604 8

1 3 5 7 9 10 8 6 4 2
2010 2012 2014 2013 2011

Printed in Great Britain by MPG Books, Bodmin, Cornwall

PREFACE

THERE is no more peaceful spot on earth than an English garden, and for some years you and I have been building up our little flower gardens, making them more beautiful, more intimate, and more than ever an essential part of our homes. But grim times are with us, and under stress of circumstances we are now called on to reorganise those gardens, and turn them into munition factories; for potatoes and beans are munitions of war as surely as are bullets and shells; and the gardeners of England can do much to help the nation in its hour of need. It is for this reason that my broadcast talks of late have taken on a war-time flavour, and deal mainly with the essential food crops. Even so, I have not forgotten the flowers entirely, as you will see, if you honour me by reading this, my fifth volume of broadcast talks. These talks are really intimate chats, and were not intended for publication, but the previous volumes having been well received, the publishers have asked for more, and publishers may not be denied.

For the moment potatoes, onions, carrots and so on must receive our full attention; but we may look forward to the time when this nightmare will end, as end it must—and the morning will break with all our favourite flowers to greet us once more, and, who knows, perhaps my next volume of talks will be of roses, mignonette, daffodils and lilies.

C. H. M.

June, 1941.

CONTENTS

AUTUMN

September

PREPARING THE WAR-TIME GARDEN

FOR nearly ten years I have been talking about the garden, and how to keep it bright and cheerful, and many of us have learned to love and understand our flowers and take an ever-increasing interest in them, and now, unhappily, we must put them into the background for a time and turn our attention to the more serious side of gardening—the food crops.

But that doesn't mean that we must throw away every flowering plant and shrub we possess; the world is quite gloomy enough as it is, without losing the pleasant company of our garden flowers, and there is no reason why we should not still plant a few tulip and other bulbs, wallflowers and forget-me-nots, so that when the spring comes, the garden won't look too drab and dreary. There are plenty of odd spots about, especially in those small front gardens, which are of no use for vegetable growing, and might just as well be kept colourful with flowers. What it does amount to is this, that so far as it lies within our power, we should now turn over as much of the garden as possible, or as much as is suitable, to the production of vegetable crops.

Now, how are we going to set about it? Well, I suggest that the first thing to do is to think it over very carefully, and work out a scheme; there's nothing to be gained by rushing out with a spade and turning everything upside down in the first few hours; that's the sort of thing novices often do—get so zealous and enthusiastic that they knock themselves up in a couple of hours, and then have a fortnight in bed with lumbago or something. Gardening, especially kitchen gardening, if you're not used to it, can be very hard work, and if you overdo it at the outset you get tired of it, and hate the sight of a spade for ever more. On the other hand, you can get just as much interest and pleasure in growing vegetables as in growing flowers, if you go the right way to work; and what I want, above all things, is that you should not only add considerably to the nation's food supply, but enjoy doing it.

I was discussing this with a friend the other day, and he said he didn't mind growing vegetables, but he couldn't see how his little bit could be of much help to the country, because in any case he could hardly grow enough to feed his own family, much less anything to sell to other people. That's the wrong point of view; it doesn't matter about selling it. Just think for a moment, if every garden grew enough to feed its owner and his family what an enormous amount of valuable food that would amount to; it would run into thousands of tons: thousands of tons less to be bought elsewhere and to be carted from place to place. So don't despise your own small efforts, grow what you can, and the more you grow the less you'll buy, and more will be available for those who are unable to produce anything themselves. Fresh vegetables form an essential part of the nation's diet, and those grown at home are always the nicest.

For those of you who have not been growing vegetables, I would suggest that you start by surveying the garden and plan it out so as to provide as large an area as you can for vegetables—one good rectangular or square piece is much more convenient to handle than a lot of odd corners and patches. It may mean moving some of the roses and other plants to more suitable quarters to get the space clear. Keep your most valuable or favourite plants and put them in a convenient place and discard all those you can do without; but when you're clearing the ground don't burn the plants or even the weeds, stack them in a heap, and as you do so, sprinkle them with an accelerator, such as *calcium cyanamide*, or sulphate of ammonia, it helps the garden rubbish, especially soft leafy material, to rot down quickly into a good substitute for manure, and when you are ready to begin digging, you can spread it over the soil, and bury it deeply as you dig. Natural manure, I'm afraid, isn't going to be too plentiful, and we shall have to use all the substitutes we can get, but I shall deal with that later on.

Now a word about the soil; different soils require different treatment. Perhaps your garden soil is heavy or clay; if this is so, your first aim must be to make it more porous, lighter and easier to work. Some clay soils seem hopeless at first, but if you persevere you can soon improve them. Start by spreading hydrated or slaked lime over the surface at the rate of anything up to twenty-eight pounds per square rod—I shall probably use the term "rod" a good deal as a unit of measurement, so we'd better make sure that you all know what a rod is. It contains thirty square yards —thirty and a quarter to be correct—or a square rod is a square piece of land measuring five and a half yards each way. I know it's very elementary, but some of

11

you may have forgotten it since you went to school, and we shall be using the term a good deal as time goes on.

Very well, then, twenty-eight pounds of lime to a square rod; then if you have anything burnable, such as hard woody garden rubbish, make a bonfire of it, and if you can burn some of the clay itself on it, and reduce it to a powder, so much the better; the idea is to get a heap of ashes to spread over the ground, anything which has been burnt is excellent stuff for mixing with clay soil. Coal ashes or cinders are not much good, but a moderate amount of the very fine sort will help. By the way, don't leave your bonfire blazing at night or you'll have the A.R.P. people after you.

If you can pick up a load of old brick dust, or mortar rubble from a demolished building, it is excellent stuff for heavy clay soil, so are the dead leaves from the trees. Anything which helps to make the clay more porous and less sticky is good for it.

On the other hand, your soil may be light and sandy. In that case you should dig into it all the soft leafy stuff you can get, such as lawn mowings and any waste vegetation; spent hops from a brewery, if you can get such things, and of course farmyard manure, the object being to make it more spongy so that it can hold moisture better.

Get yourself a set of good tools, especially a good spade, one which suits your hand, it makes a tremendous difference to your work. All these things you can do as opportunity offers, because if you're starting at the beginning, there isn't much that you can sow or plant as late as this, so you have plenty of time to get well prepared for spring planting. I'll return to the digging question in due course.

To those of you who already cultivate a vegetable garden or an allotment, the first thing I would say is don't waste anything. An enormous amount of good stuff is wasted every autumn, either because there's too much of it, or because it's not properly harvested and stored, and in some cases not even properly gathered. If you keep the runner beans gathered, for instance, as soon as they are ready for picking, the crop will last much longer. You should never leave old tough pods on the plants to go to seed—unless you want to save the seed, of course. Get every crop harvested and stored as soon as it's ready, but don't gather it until it is ready. There's a right time for everything, and very often the successful keeping of a crop depends on its being harvested in good condition at the right time.

Onions are a most valuable winter vegetable—we don't get half enough. A couple of baked onions, a roast potato and a bit of bacon make a grand meal for a winter evening. Once upon a time, when I lived alone, I used to bake onions in a tin, with a bit of dripping on the top of each, and a piece of cheese between them, and you could smell them half a mile away. There are many excellent ways of cooking onions, and they're good for you, but first you must make sure of the crop.

The first thing to do is to loosen them by gently prising them up a little with a fork, at the same time bending the tops over towards the north so that full sun can get at them to ripen them. After a week or so pull them up altogether and lay them out to dry, turning them over occasionally. The ideal way to ripen them is to give them three or four days in the shade, and then three or four days in the sun, but that, of course, isn't always possible. When they are nicely dry, and the outer skin crackles, cut the dead or dying tops off, leaving about four inches, then bind them to pieces of stick or lengths of rope and hang them up in a cool dry shed ; they keep well like that, and you can get at them easily. Don't put them in the spare bedroom, or a warm place, they prefer to be cold, but not damp—damp is the great enemy.

If you can pick up a few plants of Scotch kale, or cottager's kale, or purple sprouting broccoli, plant them out; it's a bit late, but not too late. They stand well through the winter, and blossom forth into new growth in the early spring, just when green stuff is wanted. We shall be very glad of any green stuff we can get in late February or March. But don't coddle them by deep digging or manuring. That's all right in the spring, with the summer before you, but not now. You don't want a lot of soft tender growth before the winter, it's better for them to settle down and establish themselves before the hard weather comes. A little sprinkling of lime and firm planting suits them better at this time of the year.

October

MORE PREPARATIONS

A FRIEND of mine, who is one of the latest converts to the Dig for Victory campaign, has decided to turn his garden over to the growing of food crops, and I am supposed to be lending him a hand. At the moment he is full of enthusiasm, and is slogging away at it with a stockaxe like a navvy, and my only fear is that he will overdo it and knock himself up, leaving me to do most of the rough work, which is not exactly my pet hobby.

Perhaps I ought first to describe his garden, and what we propose to do with it. It is a rectangular garden, surrounded by a shapeless old privet hedge, most of the centre part is lawn, and the rest is made up of old overgrown laurels and other bushes, some of them half-dead, two or three sprawling old decrepit apple trees, and some ancient rambler roses; you never saw such a conglomeration of rubbish in your life. I daresay there are a good many gardens up and down the country in similar condition. Well, there was never a greater opportunity or inducement to put them in order than there is to-day. What we intend to do is to make a clean sweep of the lot, grubbing out all the trees and shrubs, which won't be any sacrifice at all, make a path down the centre with a flower border each side of it, and a row of trained fruit trees behind them; leaving a little bit of lawn near the house for rest and recreation, and devote the whole of the two sides to vegetables. There are a lot of old stones about, so we propose to take the garden seat to the far end of the path and build a bit of a rockery round it. It looks very nice and sensible on paper, whether it will ever materialise is another matter. I will report progress at a later stage; if it works out according to plan it should set free about twenty rods of good ground for vegetable growing which so far has grown nothing worth while.

We made a start the other day by grubbing out an old apple tree. Now I have a great respect for old apple trees, especially if they are good old apple trees, and produce crops of useful apples, and I should be the last to want to destroy a good one; apples are valuable food, and we shall need all we can get, but I cannot see any point in keeping worn-out old trees which are half-dead and cankered, covered with moss and lichen, and only produce a few spotty-looking sour apples about every other year. If they were in an old orchard, I might try to clean them up and get them into bearing condition again, but I don't think they are worth garden room, where they cover and overshadow far too much valuable space. It seems to me much better to plant cordons or espaliers, which take up practically no room, are easily controlled and kept tidy, and produce the finest quality apple. That, at any rate is what we intend to do, but we haven't got that far yet, as I said we started to grub out an old tree.

My friend set about it early in the morning with an axe, and chopped the tree down close to the ground, leaving only the stump to be removed. That was mistake number one, as we soon discovered; the stump of a big old apple tree is a stubborn thing, it's been there a long time and doesn't give up its position without a struggle. When you are getting flabby and fiftyish you don't swing a stockaxe quite so easily as you used to do, especially if you are out of condition, with soft hands and muscles, as mine appear to be. It doesn't take much hard work to lay me out, or it didn't. I am getting a bit more used to it now and finding that the more you do the more you are able to do, provided you set about it in a rational manner. And here I would like to offer a word of advice to all middle-aged men who are about to start gardening for the first time. It need not be hard work, but you can easily make it so, and it is very often a case of more haste less speed.

I think I ought to tell you about Uncle Richard when he got the gardening fever last year—it's a warning. He had never done much of it before and he is not built on athletic lines. There is rather more of him than there used to be, and the recent additions are not so high as they might be, either in quality or altitude. He was gazing at his mangy looking lawn when I called to see him. "Not exactly velvety, is it?" he said, "what would you do about it?" I told him I should dig it up and plant potatoes on it, being war-time. He thought this a great idea and got quite enthusiastic about it. A few days later I called again; a deep brown stain disfigured the pavement and half the roadway, and the neat gravel path was scored with wheel marks and littered with blackened straw. I followed the trail round to the back garden, passed a coat and waistcoat hanging on a tree, and came upon a scene which looked rather like a bomb crater, with Uncle Richard, stripped to his shirt and steaming in the middle of it. As I approached he was bending down with the less distinguished part of his anatomy towards me. I don't know whether he was

17

looking for buttons, but we couldn't find them. "I just want to get up as far as that tennis socket," he said, "then I'm going to have a cooler and a cup of tea."

I looked in again a week later and found just the same scene, but Uncle Richard was missing. Then I heard sighs coming from the front sitting room: he was having his back poulticed. This done, I helped him, by painful degrees, to his couch near the window, where we looked at the lawn he'd ruined, and Uncle Richard said he never wanted to see a spade again, but he called it a good deal more than a spade.

There's a moral in this, which is intended specially for those of you who are not accustomed to digging or other hard work. Don't, especially in November, start off at it like a terrier digging for a rat. Take it easy until you get used to it. Do a little at a time for a start, don't keep on till you are wet through with sweat and your back feels as if it is breaking. You'll only have to pay the penalty if you do. You ought to watch Henry digging. He looks terribly slow and methodical as he quietly turns over a little at a time. I can do twice as much in half an hour, but at the end of the day it's the other way about, and while I am aching all over and thoroughly tired, he is as fresh as when he started. This is simply because he keeps quietly on without over-exerting himself, which is the golden rule that all new gardeners would do well to follow. If you do it that way you will enjoy the work and benefit by it, instead of making an ordeal of it.

But about that apple tree stump, it took us all day to excavate round the roots, and get it out bit by bit. The next one we tackled in a different way, we sawed the top off about six feet above the ground, then dug round the roots, and having six feet of trunk to lever it about with, we soon loosened it and had it out within an hour. A small point, perhaps, but one worth remembering if you've never grubbed out a tree before. Apple-wood makes very good logs for burning, so there ought to be a great saving of coal this winter. Also apple-wood is what mallets used to be made of in the old days, as it is very hard, so if any of you want a good mallet for driving posts or wedges, cut out a piece of the right diameter and put an ash stick into it, and it will last you for years. However, going back to this uprooting business, many of you who are grubbing out shrubs or trees like this, make sure that you get all the roots out, they will only prove a nuisance if you leave them in the ground. We find in that garden I was speaking of that the roots of the old privet hedge have spread themselves out a bit, so we are chopping them all off with a sharp spade about a foot away from the hedge. As we clear the ground we are giving it a good dressing of lime, and also spreading all the available autumn leaves and rubbish over it. Later on we hope to get a few loads of stuff from a neighbouring farm, and if all goes well we ought to get the ground into good condition for sowing and planting in the spring. It will probably take all the winter at the rate we are going, but that doesn't matter. It's the winter cultivation that the land wants to produce good results in spring.

Soon we shall have to be planning out the crops, and deciding which of the vegetables are the most profitable to grow, and in what proportions. I daresay many of you have made notes as to which crops have paid

19

you the best. I suppose we must put potatoes on the top of the list. I have many a time said that we could very well leave potatoes to the farmer, and in normal times I should still say so, but in view of possible transport difficulties, I think we ought to grow as many as possible at home next year, to make sure of a supply. With a good store of potatoes available we should always be sure of something welcome to eat. For the same reason, that of saving transport, I think we all ought to save, as far as possible, at least a part of our seed potatoes for spring planting, provided the crop was good and free from disease; it's no use saving seed from a poor crop. I don't think we can lay down any hard and fast rules as to which are the best vegetables to grow, it depends a lot on individual circumstances; it's no use eating cabbage if it merely gives you indigestion. For growing children or people who are actively employed, the root crops, carrots, swedes, parsnips and beetroots are excellent, as well as all the other vegetables, but for older people and those who live sedentary lives, I believe the vegetables which grow above the ground are better than those which come from below it. However, I mustn't try to set myself up as a food authority. I don't know enough about it. But I think we should be safe in making our plans if we included more onions and carrots, leeks and beans, which are good for everybody, with a good supply of potatoes, spinach and salads. The choicer, but perhaps less bulky things, such as peas, I must leave to your own discretion. But now is the time to be thinking it over, and make notes of the different vegetables while you can still remember what has happened this year. If gardeners would keep more records and notes of their successes and failures they would find them very helpful. We often repeat the same old mistakes year after year just because we have forgotten all about them when the spring comes round again.

By the way, an allotment holder the other day asked me why he couldn't lift his parsnips, which are in the way of his digging operations. He reminded me that I had once told him to store the other roots but to leave the parsnips out of doors and use them as required. I daresay I did, but I didn't intend it to be taken too literally. There is no need to store parsnips, the frosty weather actually improves the flavour, but that doesn't mean that you must leave them where they are. If they are in the way you can lift and store them like other roots, or you can dig them up and pack them close together upright in a trench in a corner of the garden, where they will improve in condition. It wouldn't be a bad idea to save a couple of good healthy looking parsnips for planting in the spring to produce a crop of seed. I don't say that it will be necessary, but you never know.

November

MAKING A START

I WAS watching a man digging the other day, turning up the turf between his apple trees in a small orchard. You ought to have seen him, he had all the symptoms of violent war-time gardening fever, and seemed to be trying to cover or uncover as much ground as possible in a short time. He was stripped to the waist, and was turning the ground over in great spadefuls as if his very life depended on it. It may do, for all I know, but he wasn't setting about it in what I call a workman-like manner. He was certainly breaking up the ground, but after he had finished you could see lumps of grass and weeds sticking out all over it. It looked rather as though a few pigs had been routing it over, and if I'm not very much mistaken, it will be just as bad as ever in about a month's time, and he'll have to do it all over again, and I can only hope that he won't get a violent chill in his lumbar regions to prevent him carrying on with it. No, my dear friends, however enthusiastic you may be that is not the way to do it. There is no need to get excited over it. If you are breaking up new ground, you are not likely to plant anything on it till the spring, so there is ample time, and it's far better to do a little each day or each week-end, and do it thoroughly. "Hasten slowly" is a golden rule when you are digging new ground. The old country gardener may seem slow, but he gets through the work much quicker than the enthusiastic amateur who works like a maniac for ten minutes and then sits down to survey his efforts for fifteen. Bury all the turf upside down as

22

deeply as possible; pick out every bit of root you can find of such pernicious weeds as couch-grass, thistles, docks, and bellbine, it's no use merely turning them over and transplanting them. If you get the ground thoroughly clean now you will save yourself endless trouble in the spring, and you won't find the work nearly so hard and fatiguing. Another friend told me that while he was digging, he kept coming across great fat white grubs, curled up in a semicircle, and almost as thick as your little finger. He didn't know whether to destroy them or not, thought they might be good friends. He showed me one; it was a cockchafer grub, known in many parts of the country as "Joe Bassett," and one of the nastiest things you can get in the soil, especially if you get them in any quantity; they chew up the roots of almost any plant, and I have seen even beds of roses killed by them. Unfortunately they are very difficult to deal with, because you can't get at them. I hope there are not many of them about this year, but I would advise you to keep your eyes open for them while digging; they are fairly easy to see as you turn the soil over, so destroy every one you can find. Another pest which is often trouble-some on new ground is the wireworm. Do you know a wireworm when you see it? It is a little thin yellow chap about half an inch long, tough and wiry, and without noticeable legs, and it can do a lot of damage to the roots of vegetable crops. Its natural home is in the turf, so when you turn over the turf into the bottom of your trench, sprinkle a little powdered naphthalene over it before you cover it with soil. You needn't throw it about in handfuls, just the lightest possible sprinkling is enough, wireworms find it very objectionable, and

23

it annoys them tremendously. At the same time, whenever you see one, take the trouble to pick him up and destroy him. It may seem a finnicky business, but it's well worth while; every one you destroy now may mean a family less sooner or later.

I'm sorry to talk about troubles, but we can't get away from them in a garden, and the sooner we tackle them the better, so in response to a great many inquiries, I'm going to say a few words about the club-root disease of the brassica, or cabbage family, which seems to be enemy number one in many vegetable gardens. Club-root disease is the indirect result of taking a plant from its natural element, or natural soil, and trying to grow it under quite different conditions. We have two very different, almost opposite types of soil in this country. The chalky or limestone soils, and the acid or sour soils, and what grows well on one, won't as a rule grow well on the other. Rhododendrons, for instance, grow well on the acid soils, but they won't grow on the chalk. Now all our brassica vegetables, the cabbages, kales, cauliflowers and so on, have a common wild ancestor, which grows naturally on the chalky cliffs and hills. It follows then that all this family need chalky or limey soils if they are to be successful (chalk and lime, by the way, mean the same thing, so far as we are concerned), and when we grow them on acid soils something is sure to go wrong. It's rather like capturing a young lion and trying to feed him on hay or carrots, it wouldn't answer. Club-root is a fungus disease which thrives in acid soils, and it doesn't like lime, so what we have to do, where the cabbages are concerned, is to convert their acid soil into a limey or

24

chalky soil and the cabbages will thrive, but the club-root fungus won't. This can be done with lime and perseverance, but it's a rather slow process. You can't stampede or hurry the action of lime, and it's no use putting huge quantities on the ground and expecting it to act immediately. The best way is to use the finely powdered hydrated lime, at the rate of a pound to a square yard, or twenty-eight pounds per square rod. Spread it over the soil and lightly fork it in, there is no need to bury it deeply; do this about a fortnight before you plant, and continue to do so each time you plant out cabbages or winter greens. Gradually the disease will get less and finally disappear altogether, but it usually takes three or four years to get rid of it. By the way, when you examine the swollen and crippled roots of attacked plants, it is quite common to find little white grubs in them, and this often gives rise to the idea that the grub is responsible for club-root. It certainly can cause swellings, but not club-root, but it seems to prefer the diseased roots to the healthy ones, and that is why you so often find it there.

Now let us turn for a moment to something a little more interesting, flowers. They will soon be getting scarce, in the garden, so we ought to make the most of what we have. Late rosebuds, for instance, if you cut them as soon as they show colour, and bring them indoors, will usually open out into perfect blooms, whereas out of doors they often fail to develop as the autumn closes in. I have often had lovely roses indoors in December by cutting them in the bud stage. Gather all the so-called everlasting flowers you can find, anything which will keep in the dried state, and hang them upside down in the shed for the time being. The winter cherries, or physalis, which produce the sprays of orange-scarlet bladders with a cherry inside, are particularly cheerful during the winter months; the silvery pods of honesty, even the ornamental seed-pods of poppies and other flowers, are all worth keeping. If you have any autumn tinted foliage, especially beech leaves, try to preserve a few for the winter; it is quite easy. If you cut smallish sprays of beech leaves before the leaves begin to drop, peel the lower part of the stems for about four inches, and split them at the bottom, and then stand them in jars of two parts water to one part crude glycerine, pack a whole bunch of stems into one jar, and leave them till they have sucked it nearly dry, they will keep quite fresh and nice through the winter, and need not be kept in water. This is much easier than putting them under the mattress and sleeping on them, as some people do. And let's be careful where we get our beech sprays and our rights in the matter. I don't want to be blamed for encouraging anyone to deface beech trees on other people's property. I know that terrible mutilations occur, especially in public places like Burnham Beeches.

And if you have none of these things, not even a garden, let me appeal to you to buy a bunch of flowers whenever you can afford it. Money spent on flowers, in moderation, is never wasted. Those chrysanthemums or carnations you see in the shops just now represent a whole year of patient labour and waiting on the part of the nursery growers. Many of them will now put their flowers into the background, and devote their energies and their greenhouses mainly to the production of food crops. It costs money to do this, and it is very necessary that they should be able to sell the flowers they have already produced, so that the money you spend on flowers will not only be supporting a deserving industry which is already feeling the pinch, but it will be helping, indirectly, towards the production of food. Besides, there are other good reasons why we should try to keep our living rooms cheerful with a few flowers. I don't think I'm a sentimental sort of person, but I am very fond of flowers. I seem to feel better and work better with a vase of flowers in front of me, and I miss them if they are not there. Perhaps there is a sort of understanding between us. I don't know; but the older I get the more I am convinced that flowers are here for something more than the mere production of seeds. Of all the wonders of science and invention during the past generation, there is still nothing quite so wonderful as the life of a flower. If we look for it, and sometimes if we don't, we find a soothing and compensating influence in flowers during times of stress and anxiety. They seem to be a link between ourselves and the Great Architect who designs them, and remind us of the better influences which even a war can't take away from us.

But to return to the food question. Get all the potatoes lifted now as soon as possible, and examine them and sort them over very carefully before you put them away. I've seen several crops lifted lately, and I find there are a lot of bad ones among them due to blight, and if these are stored with the sound ones, the trouble is likely to spread. I should also advise raking up all the haulms, or tops, and burning them at once. I don't usually advise burning waste vegetation. I would rather rot it down or dig it in as manure, but diseased potato tops are an exception; they might carry over the disease to another year if left lying about, they are safer burnt out of the way.

roots, not tough stringy ones, and big juicy leaves. In fact all our vegetables are in a sense exaggerated or over-developed, and take far more from the soil than their wild ancestors do. So we add to their living space and their food supply by loosening the soil below them and rendering more of it fertile, and as we take them away and eat them, we must also add supplies of plant food to replenish that which the crops have used and taken away. Digging, then, deepens the soil and makes more of it, it aerates it, drains away stagnant water, and enables the roots to go down deeper in search of moisture and other good things. After a period of cultivation, instead of a thin crust of good soil on the surface we have added another foot or more to it, and more than doubled its value and output. Digging is an art like anything else and we haven't all served quite as stern an apprenticeship as the older generation did. I will give you one or two tips. Good digging means breaking up and loosening the soil as deeply as possible, but it doesn't mean turning up the lower subsoil to the surface and burying the top soil down below, that does more harm than good. Start off by digging a trench, at least a foot wide and a good spade depth, then fork up the bottom of the trench to loosen it, throw into the trench all the weeds and rubbish. If you are digging grass land, skim off the turf, and turn it grass down into the bottom of the trench; then turn over the soil from one side of the trench to the other, but keep an open trench all the way through your work; if the trench gets filled up you will find the job very awkward. Don't take too much at a spadeful, you don't get on any faster, and merely make hard work of it. If you are

30

not used to digging, stop as soon as you feel the first sign of backache, and do something else. Much the best is to do a little at a time till you get used to it, otherwise you may find it a painful ordeal. Don't attempt to put a nice finish to it, leave the surface rough and lumpy, the rougher the better, so that the winter weather can penetrate deeply and sweeten it. The frost will break it up for you.

But digging alone is not enough. We also have to keep up the supplies of plant foods which are used up by the various crops. And if we were to follow a simple rule, or if we *could* follow it, we shouldn't go far wrong; that rule is to put back into the soil the equivalent of what we have taken from it, not merely in the chemical sense, but also in weight or bulk as far as we can. Years ago, when there was plenty of honest to goodness farmyard or stable muck to be had, this was a simple enough matter, we just dug a load or two of it into the soil, and it gave us what we wanted. In these days of motor-cars we can't get half enough of it, so we have to fall back on substitutes, and the substitutes very often take the form of artificial fertilisers in powder form, and that's where I want to offer a word of warning. These fertilisers can, and do, supply the necessary plant food elements in concentrated form, but they are of very little use unless the soil is in a healthy condition, and able to make use of them, and prepare them for the crops. To do this properly, the soil needs certain other things, such as air and moisture: that's where deep digging comes in; but one of the most important ingredients is *humus*, which is the residue of decaying vegetation or organic matter in the soil. Humus

31

is very often lacking, especially in sandy soils, and it should always be supplied with any system of manuring. It keeps the soil spongy, and helps it to hold moisture in dry weather, but above all it feeds the soil bacteria which prepare the plant foods from the raw materials. Farmyard manure supplies humus in just the right form, but artificial fertilisers don't supply it at all, so where we use them we must also dig into the ground plenty of waste vegetable matter, household refuse, straw, autumn leaves, seaweed, lawn mowings, or some such living material which will rot down in the soil, then we shan't go far wrong. Very well, then, assuming that the soil is well dug and stocked with humus, and has its necessary quota of lime, the next thing is to supply the actual plant foods. We know within a little the kind of chemical elements plants need as food; there are quite a number of them: iron, sulphur, magnesium, nitrogen, potash, phosphoric acid and several others, and although they need very, very little of some of them, they won't thrive without it. Fortunately most of them are nearly always present in the soil, and the only three which commonly get used up and have to be replenished are nitrogen, potash and phosphoric acid, and, of course, calcium, which is the Sunday name for lime.

Generally speaking, nitrogen is the element which produces growth, new shoots, leaves and soft tissues. It is supplied by sulphate of ammonia, nitrate of soda, nitrochalk and others, as well as by certain organic substances such as dried blood and fish manure. Potash is the element which gives us flavours, colours and quality, and does other useful work. It is supplied by sulphate

32

of potash, potash salts, kainit and, to a small extent, by the ashes of wood or rubbish which has been burnt.

Phosphoric acid or phosphates build up the woody parts of plants, ripen seeds, and generally bring the crop to maturity, and also help seeds to germinate quickly and stimulate good root action, so you see how necessary it is to have a properly balanced ration for plants, consisting of all these three in proper proportions. If you gave them nothing but nitrogen, you would get quick, sappy and tender growth, but not much else; on the other hand, if a plant got nothing but phosphates, it probably wouldn't grow at all.

Here is a suggested ration of fertilisers for an ordinary ten-rod allotment plot or kitchen garden covering the same area. During digging operations in autumn and winter give a dressing of twenty pounds of sulphate of potash, and thirty pounds of superphosphate. You may have to use a little less of these, it just depends whether the supply is equal to the demand; there may be difficulties. If you can't get sulphate of potash, you may be able to get potash salts, and instead of superphosphate you could use finely ground bonemeal. Spread it over the soil while digging, if you like, so that it gets mixed with it; it doesn't evaporate or get lost, and will still be there as required throughout the growing season. In the spring, at sowing or planting time, give a dressing of ten to fifteen pounds of sulphate of ammonia to the ten-rod plot, and repeat the dose later in the season, while the crops are growing. It's no use putting sulphate of ammonia on now, it will all be gone before the spring if you do, it acts very quickly, and should be applied when the crops are there

33

to use it. It is difficult to make definite rules, because the ration has to be varied according to the crop. For instance, leafy, quick-growing plants like spinach, which never reach maturity, require more nitrogen, or sulphate of ammonia, and less of the others, whereas if you wanted to ripen a crop of seeds you would need more superphosphate. To meet this difficulty many firms now prepare special fertilisers for the different plants, which are blended according to the plants' requirements, and some of them are well worth using. As a rule, they give directions as to quantities to use, and I'm not sure that you wouldn't do better to use these instead of mixing them yourselves. Apart from those I have mentioned, a great many substances are used as manure, both organic and inorganic. Organic, in case you've forgotten, means anything which has been prepared from animal or vegetable remains, such as dried blood, bone meal, fish manure and so on, and most of them are good and fairly safe to use, especially by beginners. Any of the fish manures are good, but they should be used in the early spring, not now. I am often asked about poultry manure, which seems to be fairly plentiful in some districts. Poultry manure is excellent stuff, and there are some very good fertilisers made from it. You can use it either dry, in the form of a powder, at the rate of twenty pounds per square rod as a spring dressing, but I think it is better when it's mixed with plenty of straw or other vegetable matter. You remember I was telling you about making a compost heap of all the waste material and garden rubbish? Well if I kept chickens I should add the droppings to that compost heap as they became available, and let the whole lot rot down together. The best place for a compost heap like that is in a pit in a corner of the garden, where it can accumulate till the autumn, and if you add poultry manure to that, by the end of a year you will have a valuable heap, practically as good as that from the farmyard. Of course, if you've got that cottage pig we've heard about, then you're on clover and should be able to grow anything. I'm afraid this has been a rather dry subject for Sunday: I would rather talk about roses, but these matters have to be discussed, and it's no use dodging them.

November

AUTUMN REMINDERS

How's the allotment looking? Not too spick and span, I hope. At this time of the year I rather like to see an allotment or vegetable plot in a rather untidy condition, with a few heaps of manure about; dead leaves and rubbish spread over it, all ready for the autumn digging, apart, of course, from the winter green crops, which should always be kept trimmed up and tidy. What about the spring cabbages, have you got a nice bed planted out yet? It's high time you had, but if you haven't, don't delay any longer. Get good plants if you can, with plenty of roots on them, not miserable little half-starved yellow things such as I have seen people planting lately. Poor old cabbages, there are a good many jokes cracked about them, but they are a jolly good standby in the garden, and we may be very glad of them in the late spring. You may not believe it, but the most difficult period in the vegetable garden is late May and early June. The winter store is practically exhausted, and the summer crops haven't arrived. In big gardens they are usually cutting asparagus, but you don't get much from allotments then, except the good old spring cabbage which holds the fort till the peas and things arrive. So again I say, make sure of a supply as quickly as you can. Another vegetable to be remembered now is the broad bean. Not one of the most economical, perhaps, but it makes a pleasant change, especially if you can get it early, before the first crop of peas arrives. After that broad beans are not so much appreciated. The way to get an early crop is to sow them now, they are perfectly hardy and stand well through the winter, and in the spring they race ahead and come into bearing much earlier than those sown in the spring, and they don't get the black fly nearly so bad. The best way to sow them now is to rake the soil down to a nice tilth, then stretch your line across, and just push the seeds into the ground six inches apart all along it; then another similar row a foot away from it. After sowing, pull the soil over the seeds with a hoe to form a little ridge a good inch high along each row; this is better than sowing them in drills as you do in the spring, especially if the soil is inclined to be wet during the winter. You nearly always lose a few, so it is just as well to sow a few more somewhere else, to fill up any gaps which occur. Be careful where you put these beans, and see that they fit into the cropping scheme, or they may be in the way of more important crops when the time for spring sowing comes round. The long-pod varieties of broad beans are the best for autumn sowing.

Now a few words about fruit trees; there seems to be a little misunderstanding about as regards the planting of apples, pears and plums. Obviously, if you plant trees now you are not going to get immediate returns from them, and it is quick returns we are looking for at the present time. But if you want to plant a few new ones, there is nothing to prevent you doing so, and for the sake of the nursery trade, I hope you will carry out any plans you may have made in that direction, always bearing in mind that quick-growing food crops are of the first importance.

Actually I think many of us might well reorganise our fruit trees with considerable benefit to the garden

B *

as a whole, by doing away with some of the big over-grown trees, which cover a considerable area, and planting small ones, such as cordons, of better varieties. In my opinion there are far too many early varieties about, especially of apples; this year has demonstrated that fact very conclusively. Many people have had so many early apples that they could neither eat them, sell them, or give them away, and, of course, they are of no use for storing. Take my own case as an example. In my small garden I planted two trees of early varieties. Gladstone and Worcester pearmain. I did it because I like to see a tree of rosy apples, and also to pick one ripe from the tree in the summer, but at the moment I wish they were good keeping apples. In a heavy cropping year like this, it has been very difficult even to give them away. The Gladstones dropped all over the place, they were swarming with birds and wasps, and even the good ones were soft and mushy long before we could use them. When the tree has only about a dozen on it, we appreciate them, but in an abundant year waste seems to be unavoidable. So it seems to me that it would be quite a sound and economical plan to grub out these two trees, which would set free a considerable space of ground and let more sunshine into the garden; and at the same time plant a row of cordons, or half a dozen bush trees of carefully selected varieties which would spread the supply over as long a period as possible. I shall return to the subject presently, and suggest a few good varieties.

Now what are you going to do about roses this year? I cannot imagine any good English garden in peace or war without its roses, so if you find it necessary to turf out some of the old ones to make room for vegetable crops, I hope you'll plant some new ones somewhere else, wherever you can find convenient room for them. There are splendid stocks available this year in the nurseries, and I'm afraid many of them will have to be destroyed unless we buy a few as usual. It must be very hard for a man who has devoted his life to roses to have to sacrifice acres of them and grow potatoes instead; but war is full of hardships, and that's what many of them will have to do, and knowing the rose growers as I do, I'm pretty sure they will do it cheerfully, without snivelling and grousing about it; but if we *can* buy a few trees, it will ease their burdens a little, and we shall be glad of the roses when the summer comes. Where space is restricted, and the flower borders limited, you could plant standards here and there among the other plants; they would then stand up well above the other flowers without taking up any room. I expect we shall have to put all sorts of mixtures in the flower borders now; the borders, in many cases, will be very much reduced in size, but that's all the more reason why they should be filled with just the very best of things, and make up in quality what they lack in quantity.

A friend of mine has a small lean-to glasshouse, which is more in the nature of an enclosed verandah, or a tiny conservatory than anything else. The dining or living room opens into it, and he wants to know if it's possible to grow anything in the vegetable line in it during the winter. It isn't heated, but it gets a certain amount of warmth from the house; during the summer he has grown tomatoes in it, I believe a good many houses have similar little glass structures attached to them, and although I'm afraid they are not of great value for vegetable growing, there are a few things you might try. Salads, for instance; you could grow boxes of mustard and cress, all you want for that are flat boxes half full of ordinary potting soil, made nice and level on the surface. You then spread the seed thickly all over it, and press it down flat to the soil with a piece of wood or a flat iron; gently, of course, so that all the seeds are touching the soil, but don't cover them with soil; then put a pane of glass over the box, and a sheet of newspaper over that till the seeds have germinated, then remove the paper and the glass by degrees as the mustard and cress grows up. Mustard grows quicker than cress, so they shouldn't be mixed together; it's better to sow the cress two days before the mustard. You can also grow lettuce like this, and very nice it is, too. Cos or tall lettuce is the best. You sow the seed in boxes, the same as mustard and cress, but in the case of lettuce it is better to cover the seeds lightly with fine soil. Then when the young lettuce plants are three or four inches high, you cut them all down and eat them as they are. You can also sow white Lisbon onions in boxes for use in salads, during the winter, while they are young and tender, and you can sow a box of cauliflowers, *All the Year Round* is a good variety; transplant them as they grow, and keep them light and airy, and plant them out of doors in the spring, and you will get some nice early heads. In the late winter and early spring, you can sow all sorts of things in a small house of that description: onions, peas, beans, celery, marrows and so on for planting out later, but we'll talk about them later on. There is just one tip I would like to give you. When you are filling boxes with soil for seed sowing, mix a little superphosphate with the soil, about a teaspoonful to an average seed-box; it makes a wonderful difference to the germination of seeds, and be careful with the water. Young seedlings want enough, but you can very easily give them too much. The best way is to hold the box in a bath of water and allow the water to percolate up from the bottom, without wetting the seedlings, this is better than watering overhead. Another thing you can do in a little greenhouse is to prepare a dark corner under the stage somewhere, so that you can do a little forcing later on, and it might be worth while to dig up a few roots of mint and put them in a box in the greenhouse. You would get an early supply then to make mint sauce for the Easter lamb. And remember that all these things which can be grown in a cold greenhouse, can also be grown in a garden frame if you have one, so don't let it stand empty and idle.

November

AMONG THE FRUIT TREES

Now let us talk about fruit and the necessity for keeping up the supply as far as possible. I have, on more than one occasion since the war began, advocated the grubbing out and scrapping of old fruit trees to make room for other and more urgent food crops, but I don't want to be misunderstood. The trees I want to see scrapped are those useless but picturesque old specimens which sprawl about the garden, occupying a great deal of room, but producing nothing of any value. Such trees are better out of the way, but that doesn't mean we should stop planting fruit trees; rather, I think, we should aim at increasing the supply, and whenever a worn-out or overgrown old tree is removed I would like to see a few young ones, of better varieties, planted in its stead. We mustn't get the idea that fruit is an unnecessary luxury; it isn't, it is an essential part of our national diet, especially apples. For many years we have been pushing ahead with the eat more fruit campaign, and people have responded to it, and during recent years the consumption of fruit has increased by leaps and bounds, and the general health of the public has improved as a result. If Darwin's theory is correct, our earliest ancestors lived almost entirely on fruit, and now that we seem to be drifting back towards the original state again, we shall probably need more fruit than ever, so that history can repeat itself, and bring us back to the paths of sanity and civilisation. The objection to planting fruit trees in war-time is that they take some time to produce a crop, and in these urgent times we have to turn our attention to food crops which will give us quick returns. A very reasonable objection too; but there is no need to overdo it; fruit is essential, and space could be found in nearly every garden, and even on permanent allotments, for a few trees or bushes, without interfering to any extent with the vegetable crops. Of course we must remember that fruit trees are a more or less permanent feature of a garden, and plant accordingly. We must also remember that small trees have a habit of growing into big ones, and unless we plant wisely they will soon spread themselves across the garden and crowd out other essential crops; but there is no need for this if you choose the right type of trees, and keep them under control. For the small garden I always recommend trained trees, such as cordons or espaliers, which take up very little room, are easily kept under control, and usually produce the finest fruit.

Cordon and espalier apples and pears can be planted in rows, along the front of a wall or building, at the back of the vegetable plots, or as dividing fences. They occupy very little space and do not shade anything, or interfere with the growing of other crops. I expect most of you know what cordons and espaliers are, but in case some of you don't, a cordon is just a straight stem without branches, which is encouraged by a special system of pruning, which I shall explain in a minute or two, to produce fruit along its entire length, instead of shoots and branches. It doesn't take up much more room than a good sized hollyhock, and can be attended to conveniently without steps or ladders. I know one old gentleman who prunes his cordons comfortably seated on an old shooting stick, so they are

43

ideal trees for cripples or old people. They can be planted in a row, two feet apart, and tied to a wire or to strong stakes. They are usually planted sloping at an angle of forty-five degrees, instead of upright. Some gardeners slope them towards the north, others towards the south. There is something to be said for both ideas, but personally, I prefer to slope them to the south, if possible, because if they are pointing towards the sun they don't shade each other so much. It isn't a strong point, however. The real reasons for sloping them are that you can get a longer tree in a given height, for instance, on a six-foot fence you can have trees eight or nine feet long. But a more important reason is that the sloping position retards the flow of sap, and encourages the production of fruit along the lower half as well as the upper. If you plant them upright they have a tendency to make a bush of strong growth at the top, and gradually become bare towards the bottom. The espalier is a trained tree with a central upright stem, and a series of horizontal branches on each side of it, one above the other. It is a nice tree to look at, particularly so in an old walled kitchen garden, but it is not so easily managed, so for the gardener of limited experience I would recommend cordons. They can be bought ready made, three years old, from any good nursery, and will start bearing fruit next year if you want them to, or you can buy maiden trees budded last year, and train them yourselves. You must get trees which are budded on to the dwarfing, or Paradise crab stock. If they are on strong stocks, such as are used for large trees, you will find it difficult to restrict the growth and keep them within bounds. This, I admit, is a matter for the nurseryman, and you would be well advised to go to a reliable firm, where proper stocks are used: to buy cheap trees from an unknown source is a doubtful gamble. Cordon apples and pears usually grow well in any good garden soil, provided it is well drained and doesn't get waterlogged. Naturally they prefer a deeply dug soil, but there is no need to put strong manure in it, they are better without it in their early stages. Some gardeners won't agree with me on this point, and many books advocate digging in a good dose of manure before planting; but in the case of cordons I don't agree with them. Young trees will build up a healthier root system in normal soil than in contact with strong manure, and if the diet is too rich they will make soft sappy growth with shoots a yard long. That may be O.K. if you want to build up a big tree and wait years for the fruit, but in the case of a cordon, where growth is to be restricted, it is just what you don't want. Obviously, even a cordon can't grow on a starvation diet, so you must use your own judgment and try to find the happy medium, a good average soil, avoiding extremes in either direction. The only manure I recommend at planting time is a handful of bonemeal, and an ounce of sulphate of potash if you can get it, if not, wood ashes, for each tree, thoroughly mixed with the soil. In the following summer a little strawy farmyard stuff, or even litter, laid on the surface round the trees as a mulch, will benefit them by conserving moisture and keeping the roots cool, but there is no need to dig it in.

You can plant trees any time from now to March, provided the soil is in a workable condition, but don't do so when it is wet and sticky, especially on clay, or it will go down as solid as a batter pudding. I like to get it done in November if possible, but it is not essential. When you plant a tree spread the roots out as much as possible, and plant firmly, so that it isn't easy to lift the tree out again: pack the soil round the roots a little at a time and tread it down tight. Put the stake in before the tree or you may damage the roots and loosen the tree by driving it in afterwards. Don't plant deeply, especially on heavy soil; this is a common fault with amateurs. So long as the roots are well covered and firmly anchored, the shallower they are the better, so long as they are not allowed to get dry. They must, of course, be securely staked, or the wind will loosen them. After planting give each tree a bucket of water to settle the soil round the roots.

Now a word about pruning, and remember I am talking about cordons, not about free-growing trees, which in my opinion often get far too much pruning, but more about that some other time. If you buy three-year-old cordons, ask the nurseryman to prune them for you before planting. If you start with a maiden, which is usually just a single stem, cut a little off the end, to leave it about eighteen inches to two feet long: if it has any small side shoots, cut them off. After that, pruning is much the same for either kind. During the summer young shoots will sprout out along the main stem, these are called laterals; at the same time a new shoot will appear at the top and continue the length of the main stem, this is called the leader. In July you cut off the ends of all the side shoots or laterals, leaving them about half their length, but you don't touch the leader at that time. The laterals will soon produce a new shoot

46

towards the end to take the place of the piece you cut off. In the winter, while the trees are dormant, you cut off all the side shoots, not only the bit which has grown since the summer pruning, but also the lower half which you left on, leaving only a stump of each containing two buds or leaf marks, usually about an inch. The leading shoot is also cut back a bit in the winter, about eighteen inches from where it started in the spring. This eighteen inches will be added to the length of the tree each year until it is as tall as you want it: then, instead of cutting it you bend it over to form a loop and tie it to itself. After that all new shoots are treated as laterals, and pruned in summer as well as in winter. It isn't an easy business to describe in a few words, but I hope I've made it fairly clear. The reason for cutting the laterals in the summer is that it checks the flow of sap for a time, which has a tendency to congregate in the lower buds and swell them up into fruit buds, so that they form bunches of blosson and fruit instead of new shoots. If you didn't cut them in the summer, but allowed them to grow to their full length, and then cut them back in the winter, the result would be a large number of new shoots in the spring, but little or no fruit, and your tree would soon be a dense thicket of useless growth.

And what about varieties? There are many to choose from, but some of them grow much too strongly to conform to the restricted growth of a cordon, so let us choose a few suitable ones. Tastes differ, I know, and I can only suggest what I consider the best. Someone else might recommend quite a different selection which would be quite as good as mine, but I am thinking, not only of quality, but also of general health and reliability in cropping; there is not much point in planting super varieties if you never get a crop. Let us start with dessert apples. For an early one I suggest Epicure, a delicious apple for August, to be gathered and eaten straight away. A nice September apple is St. Everard, a smallish apple which strongly resembles the famous Cox's Orange Pippin, except that it is early and doesn't keep. James Grieve is a lovely crisp, juicy apple for October; and another favourite of mine is Ellison's Orange, which has a very distinct flavour; some say it rather suggests aniseed, but it's a very nice form of aniseed. Cox's Orange Pippin is still the popular favourite, and there is nothing quite like it, but it is a bit exacting, and I wouldn't recommend it for cold districts or heavy clay soils. I would rather recommend a modern one, called Laxton's Fortune: this is a lovely apple, with a rich pine-appley sort of flavour, and one of the best I know. For Christmas I should say Superb is about the best of the bunch; it is very reliable, with a very distinct and pleasant flavour. For a later apple Orleans Reinette takes a bit of beating; it is not so well known as it deserves to be, but is an extremely nice apple.

For cooking I would suggest Early Victoria as a summer apple, Lane's Prince Albert for the autumn, and King Edward VII to keep for the winter. The popular Bramley seedling is too strong a grower for training as a cordon. Another good cooker is Crawley Beauty: I include it because it flowers a fortnight later than most of the others, and after a frosty spring it often gives a good crop when the others fail.

Of the numerous pears we have to choose from I

shall only recommend three for the amateur or in-experienced, because some of the very choice are not very reliable. Three good ones, which are of excellent quality and usually crop well, are Dr. Jules Guyot, an early yellow pear very much like a "William" but more reliable and not so scabby; Louise Bon of Jersey, a grand old pear, not very big, but of distinct flavour; and Conference, a richly flavoured late October pear, and the most reliable cropper of the lot.

WINTER

December

CASTLES IN THE AIR

I'M afraid there is nothing very exciting about allotments and gardens in the middle of December; it usually means digging or muck spreading, or gathering cold wet greens or something equally thrilling. But even a war can't prevent the spring coming and bringing the gardening fever with it, so I always think, while we are marking time in these dark days, it is quite interesting and also profitable to get a pencil and paper by the fireside after the day's work, and build a few castles in the air; work out plans for all the good things we are going to grow next summer. That, at any rate, is what I am doing just now. You remember, some weeks ago I told you about an old garden we were clearing to make room for vegetables? Well, the laurels and things have all disappeared, and all there is to see now is what appears to be a vast vacant space of soil thrown up into rough heaps and ridges, with lime scattered over it, and a goodly supply of leaves and other waste material underneath. It doesn't look at all attractive at the moment, but in my mind's eye I can already see beautiful rows of peas and spinach, beds of spring carrots, cauliflowers, lettuces and onions, and other good things which, if the dream comes true, will make all this back-aching grubbing and digging worth while.

As I said before, we propose to divide the garden by a centre path, with a three-foot flower border along each side and a row of trained fruit trees behind them. All the rest of the ground on both sides will be devoted entirely to good crops; with the possible exception of a row of sweet peas. Hitler or no Hitler, war or no war, I'm going to grow a few bunches of sweet peas next summer, if at all possible. Very naughty of me, perhaps, but I had none last summer, and I missed them terribly. After all, they don't take up much room, and to me they seem to bring a breath of Heaven down to this unhallowed earth—a message of peace, of hope and a promise of better times to come. I'm sure I should be a happier and a better man, if I could always have a bunch of sweet peas on the table in front of me.

However, the first order of to-day is food, so let us consider the vegetables. To start with we intend to divide the garden into four equal sections to simplify the cropping arrangements, putting the early crops on one, the late summer crops on another, and the winter crops on the third, so that in the next year we can change them round to ensure a good rotation. I have explained this idea so many times that I don't propose to go into details now, but it is obviously an advantage if you keep the early crops together, so that all this particular plot becomes vacant about the same time. Suppose you started sowing in the spring without any prearranged plan; the earliest sowings out of doors are broad beans, parsnips, early peas and shallots, which can all go in in February, and you might sow them all one after another on the same patch of ground. The broad beans, the early peas and the shallots would be cleared off during July, but the parsnips would have to remain there till the winter, and would prevent the ground being cleared for the next crop—obviously they should be on the same plot as the celery, runner beans and root crops, which could all carry on together till the late autumn or winter.

That, then, accounts for three of our four plots. On the fourth we are going to put the things which have to stop where they are more or less permanently, instead of rotating. We hope to plant a couple of rows each of gooseberries, currants and raspberries, and, if we can find room for it, a strawberry bed. We shall also have a few rhubarb roots, a bed of herbs and, when the war is over, we may make an asparagus bed, but that will have to wait. The compost, or rubbish heap, will have to be on this plot, too. This compost idea, as a substitute for manure, hasn't caught on quite so well as it ought to have done. In spite of blackout difficulties, there has been far too much burning of rubbish which ought to go back into the ground. A neighbour of mine started a compost heap last spring. He dug a square pit about three feet deep and piled the soil round it like a rampart; then he started putting all his rubbish and lawn mowings and the cleanings from his chicken run into it, sprinkling sulphate of ammonia over it each time he added a load. It gradually grew and grew, until he had a heap nearly six feet high, and you ought to see it now. He has been wheeling it and spreading it over the ground for digging in, a beautiful black, stinking mass, the envy of all the gardeners around. We must pay a little more attention to the compost heap next year, it pays. Perhaps some of you who dug up new ground a year ago haven't needed any manure so far, but, if you've taken good crops this year, you certainly ought to put something back into the soil now to replace the loss; and not fertilisers alone, but bulky stuff, too, if you can get it.

But to come back to our garden, and taking the early plot first, I shall start with a couple of rows of peas, four feet apart, with a row of spinach between them. These can be sown in the last week of February or early March. Some people like the dwarf peas, such as Little Marvel, English Wonder or Peter Pan, which don't need staking, but, if you can get the sticks and don't mind the trouble, I think the tall growers are nicer and more profitable. Gradus, Pilot and Foremost are three good early varieties, which grow about three feet high. Personally, I want nothing better than Gradus, and I keep sowing it at fortnightly intervals all through the summer to keep up a succession, and its quality is about as good as need be. I like to see a nice row of peas neatly staked in the garden. They seem to add tone to it. Another pea I hope to have is the sugar pea, Paramount, which I have already told you about. You let it grow full size and then eat pod and all. There isn't a bit of stringiness about it, and it is as sweet as sugar—an ideal summer vegetable for war-time economy. This won't go on the early plot because it takes longer to mature; we shall put a row on the second plot, and sow them in March. So much for peas, we mustn't overdo them; they are a bit extravagant in war-time.

The next thing for the early plot is a few rows of shallots. I usually find two rows enough, but I shall put down four this year, two of the small variety for pickling, and two of the giants, in case onions are scarce. You can often grow good shallots where you can't grow good onions. You can plant shallots as early as you like, some old gardeners say plant them on the shortest day and pull them on the longest, but I get good results by planting them in February, and find it more convenient. Then we must have a few rows of stump rooted carrots, another of nature's blessings, and some early snowball turnips, a bed of cabbage lettuces and a few radishes, three or four rows of broad beans and a couple of rows each of dwarf French beans and round beetroots. Although the French beans and round beets go on the early plot, they mustn't be sown before the middle of April at the earliest. Early vegetables really mean quick maturing vegetables; it doesn't follow that those you sow first are ready for use first. You can sow dwarf beans and peas in late April and eat them in July, whereas you sow parsnips in February and don't eat them till Christmas. The two rows of round beetroots on the early plot are intended for use during the summer while they are young and tender. We shall sow more on the other plot for winter use. We shall fill up what remains of the first plot with early potatoes, perhaps about half a dozen rows, enough to see us through the summer. Then we shall be able to clear this plot during the summer, give it a good liming, and plant out the brussels sprouts and other winter greens without intercropping or overcrowding. These will have been raised on the seed-bed on the permanent plot.

That brings us to the second plot, to produce crops for the late summer and autumn. We must plant out a bed of cabbages there, and a row or two of cauliflowers, some more round beet and short carrots, more peas and lettuces, and fill it up with early main crop potatoes. We shall bank on such varieties as Majestic, Great Scot and Ally, which crop heavily and can be lifted and stored in September. If you grow the late varieties, which have to remain in the ground till the late autumn, they very often get full of slugs and blight in October, and, if it happens to turn wet, it's a nasty mucky job lifting them. I like to be finished with potato digging by the first of October. This second plot of summer and early autumn vegetables ought to be cleared by the end of September, which gives us a nice opportunity for a bit of quiet digging before the dirty weather sets in. We shall put the main onion bed on this plot. I am hoping this year, instead of sowing seed, to get sufficient young ones for planting out in the spring, so as to be able to harvest them in September, while the sun is warm enough to ripen them well. They keep better then.

The third plot, on the other side of the path, will accommodate the root crops for the winter store; late carrots, beets, parsnips, turnips and so on; also the runner beans and the celery trench. Runner beans might be called a summer crop, but they often keep on well into the autumn, so they should be either on the late plot or along the end or side of one of the others, where they needn't be disturbed. If any part of the garden happens to be low-lying and wet, this is the place to reserve for celery, because it likes any amount of moisture. I hope to put a couple of rows of Jerusalem artichokes across the end of the late plot. I'm rather fond of artichokes as an occasional change, but they are not everybody's fancy.

That leaves us with the fourth, or permanent plot. I've got several ideas for this. In addition to the compost heap or pit, and the fruit bushes, I hope to make a nice seed-bed, where I can raise all sorts of seedlings for planting out. The essential thing about a seed-bed is a well-dug soil, with the upper part broken and raked down to a fine surface, but without strong manure in it. The only fertiliser I use on a seed-bed is superphosphate, or, as an alternative, bonemeal, about two ounces to each square yard well raked in in the spring. It gives the seedlings a good start, and I like to get them off the seed-bed as soon as possible, and transplant them to richer soil. A good seed-bed is very handy; you can raise lettuces, greens, beans and all sorts of other vegetables for filling up gaps and keeping up a constant supply. If I can get the materials, I should like to make a couple of frames, too, and, perhaps, even a little greenhouse one of these days, but perhaps that is getting a bit too ambitious for the time being. I should like to get a nice bed of herbs going; mint, thyme, sage, chives, tarragon, sweet savoury and all the rest of them. These herbs can make a tremendous difference to vegetable dishes, if you know how to use them, and they are very easy to grow. And yet, how often we find ourselves without even a handful of mint in the spring, when we could so easily have grown a bit by planting a few roots in the autumn. A good way to grow mint is to let an old bath or box into the ground, with the bottom knocked out, and plant it in that. Then it stays put, instead of wandering about among the other stuff where it isn't wanted.

January

SEED CATALOGUES

I WONDER what 1941 has in store for us, although I'm afraid it is not much use wondering, we must hope for the best and prepare for the worst. In the garden, at any rate, we must be up and doing, and aim at producing at least double the amount of food we have ever grown before. In all our cropping plans I have a feeling that we ought to concentrate more than ever on growing vegetables for next winter and spring, stuff like potatoes, onions and carrots, which can be stored to meet a possible shortage or transport difficulties. We don't usually go short of fresh vegetables in the summer and autumn, so for my part I am working out a scheme to get as much as possible to turn in after next Christmas. Anyway I hope all those of you who have a garden or an allotment will have a very successful year and get bumper crops, and not only those who have allotments, but also those who are going to have one, for I hope there is going to be a great increase in the army of allotment holders this year, especially in country villages, where there is more land available. Allotments don't look very attractive or inviting just now, do they? But they will when the crocuses begin to bloom and the gardening fever asserts itself, and it may be too late to get the one you want, so take my tip, if there is a plot going anywhere handy, snap it up now, don't hesitate any longer.

Meanwhile, the new seed catalogues are arriving, and giving me a considerable amount of pleasure and interest. I had been wondering, what with the paper shortage and the seed shortage, whether there would be any catalogues at all this year, but my mind has been set at rest on that point, they are here, and almost as good as ever. As was to be expected, prices of most seeds are a bit higher than usual, but we mustn't mind that. I think we are jolly lucky to get them at all. I take off my hat to the seed trade; it seems nothing short of a marvel to me that they are able to deliver the goods almost as usual at a time like this. Most of the seeds are usually grown on the Continent, which is now out of bounds, and in addition to that the majority of the brassica plants, such as cabbage, broccoli, brussels sprouts and such like, which were growing for seed in this country, were destroyed by frost during last winter. I should think the seed trade must have had a bit of a nightmare over it all, because you can't *make* seeds, however clever you may be, and one might well have prophesied that there would be very few seeds this year at all. But somehow, in spite of all the difficulties, the seeds are here very much as usual, so again I say, I salute the seed trade for what seems to me a wonderful piece of work.

Mind you, there may be shortages, that is unavoidable in war-time. Place your order quickly, while the going is good, and don't be greedy. Don't order a double quantity of anything, just because it happens to be scarce; order less, just as little as you need for reasonable requirements, and use it carefully. Then there may be enough to go round. We are funny people in some respects, you've only got to be told a thing is scarce, and the crowd scramble to get it, whether they really want it or not. Don't let us do that sort of thing with seeds, if we use them economically and sensibly there should be enough for us all, but not if we sow five thousand seeds to get five hundred plants, which is often done.

In villages, and where local garden societies exist, a great deal of good work could be done by sowing certain seeds in bulk. In nearly every group or association of gardeners or allotment holders there are sure to be a few experienced gardeners who possess the necessary glass accommodation for raising seedlings early and safely, or a good seed-bed in a sheltered place, and the knowledge and experience to do it. Suppose one of these undertook to raise onions for all the members, and another brussels sprouts or cabbages, celery, lettuces or leeks, as the case might be, distributing the young plants to the members all ready for planting out? Look what a saving of seed it would mean. Take onions as an example: you could make an ounce of seed go as far as half a dozen ounces would in the hands of individual members each sowing their own. There are other advantages, too. Individual members would avoid the difficulties and snags of raising their own onions; the early attacks of fly and so on; by planting out the required number no thinning would be necessary, and the chances are that a much better crop would be the result. Public spirited people often express their willingness to help the local war-time allotment movement. Perhaps they have a good garden of their own, and a gardener; they don't need an allotment themselves, and have no land to offer, and sometimes may be wondering how best they can help. Well, here is a suggestion. Offer to raise seedlings for the allotment holders, especially beginners who have had little or no experience. You could save them a great deal of trouble and disappointment, and be saving precious seeds at the same time. It only means getting together to talk it over and make the necessary arrangements. There should be no great difficulty about it. In the case of some of the more progressive allotment associations, I should rather like to see them try out the idea of a sort of communal nursery, where seedlings of all kinds could be raised in bulk for the members. It would be an interesting experiment, and ought to prove a profitable one too. It would also help to bring the allotment holders together, and anything which does that is good. That is why I am so keen on forming local associations, we can learn so much from each other if we get together and talk. I think I shall have to think out a new song for allotment holders, on the lines of the old froth-blowers' anthem, "The more we dig together, the happier we shall be."

Now let us have a look through one of these catalogues and see if there is anything of special interest. Beans look very much as usual, and there are plenty of varieties to choose from. You'll have to go a bit easy with them at half a crown and three shillings a pint, but even half a pint goes a long way if you space them out properly. Two varieties which I am glad to see in the catalogue are the haricots "White Rice" and the "Brown Dutch." These are grown for harvesting and drying, to be used during the winter instead of imported haricots, and very good they are too. We shall find a few pounds of them very acceptable next winter. If you can't get

Brown Dutch or White Rice, almost any of the dwarf
French varieties, such as Canadian Wonder, can be
grown for drying. Beetroots will be wanted, and all
the usual varieties seem to be here, including the seakale beet and the spinach beet. The spinach beet is
becoming popular, because its leaves make a good
substitute for spinach, especially during the winter.
The seakale beet is not so well known; it is rather similar
but each leaf has a thick white midrib. You eat the green
part of the leaves as spinach, cutting out the midribs
and cooking them in bundles like seakale or asparagus.
If you get your head well back and use your imagination
a bit they are not at all bad. They are grown in the
same way as ordinary beets, but you don't want many,
you can hardly call them a war-time vegetable. In the
brassica section there are some nice photographs of
cabbages, sprouts and cauliflowers, but I think we may
take them for granted, and make a note of the kales,
which are so essential for keeping the pot boiling in
April, before the spring cabbages arrive. Scotch kale
and Cottager's kale are both good and well known.
I daresay most of you have got a row of Scotch kale
now. Well, if I were you I should gather the top leaves
now, and then leave them alone till March or April.
The tops now are not so good as brussels sprouts or
savoys, perhaps, but if you pick them off you get a much
better crop of tender shoots later on. Another kale which
is not often grown is the Russian kale, useful because
it is hardy and late, and sometimes the only one left
after a very hard winter. The sprouting broccolis are
also very acceptable in the spring. You all know the
purple sprouting kind, which is surely one of the best

of early spring vegetables, but not many people seem to know the green sprouting broccoli, also known as Calabresse. This is a broccoli which produces a big head during the summer if you sow it in March. After the centre head is cut it begins to sprout out little green bunches which last well into the autumn, and the flavour is very good indeed.

Celery is not officially recommended as a war-time vegetable, but it is very acceptable during the winter, either cooked or raw, and I don't know whether you are aware of it, but some people say that celery is an excellent remedy for rheumatism, so I think rheumaticky subjects, at least, ought to have a row. We can pass over cucumbers, cardoons and capsicums, but don't forget leeks. We ought to aim at a succession of leeks this year, so that we may enjoy them all through the winter. What a lot of lettuce varieties there are nowadays, the numbers are almost confusing, so I shall leave the selection to you. The cabbage types are rather quicker, and perhaps of more delicate flavour, but there's a lot to be said for the cos, or tall growing kinds, in war-time, especially such whoppers as Jumbo and Balloon—you get more for your money.

With regard to onions, I'm afraid this year it is going to be a case of what we can get rather than what we want, but for my part I would rather have a good crop of reliable and healthy medium-sized onions than gamble with an outsize uncertainty, so I think I shall stick to Bedfordshire Champion and James's Keeping; but I've been promised some young plants of Giant Rocca for planting out in the spring, and these ought to give me the biggest bulbs.

That brings us to the potatoes, and here again there are so many varieties that I should find it extremely difficult, indeed impossible, to pick a couple from each section, early, second early, and main crop, and say that they were the best half-dozen. Majestic is a good potato in most districts. I saw some fine crops of it last year. It cooks a bit black in some places, but otherwise I have no fault to find with it, except that it is rather watery and doesn't like to be cut before planting, which is a little awkward if the seed tubers happen to be on the large size. If I were selecting a potato for a new allotment, where the ground is a bit rough, I should choose Kerr's Pink, a strong growing, heavy cropper, which is just right for cleaning and breaking up dirty land. It is a pink potato, with rather deep eyes, slightly on the coarse side as regards quality, but it will grow where a good many of the others won't. Arran Banner is another good potato, an early main crop which matures early and keeps well. What a lot of "Arrans" there are now: Arran Luxury, Arran Rose, Arran Banner, Arran Comrade, Arran Chief, Arran Pilot, Arran Peak, and all good ones too, raised by that fine Scotsman, Mr. McKelvie, of the Isle of Arran, who has devoted his life to raising new and better varieties of potatoes. I wonder whether we appreciate, as we should do, the work of such men as this, who have given us all these fine varieties, and added considerably to the nation's food supply, and also to the beauty of the garden. Think of all the lovely carnations raised by my old friend Allwood; the splendid apples raised by Mr. Laxton, to mention only a few. Very often these raisers get little out of it; there are no patents or

However, our first job is to grow them, so we had better discuss the pros and cons. Potatoes will grow in most kinds of soil, but they will grow much better in good soil with plenty of manure in it. We must always remember that they are exotics, not British plants, and they have to crowd all their work of growing and ripening into one of our short summers. So the more we can do to help them the better the results are likely to be. Now is the time to prepare the soil by digging a bit of good muck into it, if you can get it, but above all, by digging it deeply and throwing it up into loose heaps or ridges so that the weather can get into it. Hop manure, poultry manure, fish manure are all good, or you can use a good potato fertiliser in the spring. Potatoes are not exacting, so long as they have got something to bite on. But don't give them fresh lime; they like the after-effects of lime, that is, land which was limed a year ago, but fresh lime has a tendency to encourage scabby potatoes. The great thing is to keep the soil open by forking it over, especially as the spring approaches, then the warmth of the sun gets into it and makes it fit for planting earlier. I won't say anything about varieties, except to repeat that for the average garden or allotment I think the mid-season varieties such as Great Scot, Majestic and Arran Banner are better than the late ones, because you can get them up and into the store in September before the potato troubles get serious, and they produce equally heavy crops. Indeed, the biggest crop I ever saw was of Great Scot, which produced over twenty tons to the acre, while the popular King Edward on the same ground only produced nine tons. That seems to be a point worth considering in war-time, even if we have to sacrifice a little quality in the interests of quantity. Be careful where you get your seed. You may not have as much choice as usual, but get seed from Scotland or the North of England if you can, it is much better than seed grown in the South, partly because it has a shorter season there, and is lifted slightly immature, before it has time to become infected with the mysterious virus diseases which are so common nowadays. But, wherever you get it from, get it as soon as you can, before the supplies begin to get short. We know, of course, that you won't be planting potatoes for some months yet, but it is advisable to get the seed in hand well in advance of planting time, because you can do a lot for them before planting, and thus save valuable time. Getting them sprouted before planting is a great advantage, because it enables you to delay planting till the soil is ready, and the tubers will soon make rapid growth; it also enables you to control the number of shoots and get a better crop. When you receive the potatoes, set them out in a single layer in shallow trays or boxes, with the nose end of each potato upwards; the nose end is the rounded end of the tuber which contains most of the eyes; the other end is the heel end, which was attached to the parent plant. Put the trays somewhere in a light cool place. Up in the loft would do, so long as there is plenty of daylight, and it can be kept warm enough to keep the frost away. The idea is to induce them to start sprouting, but you mustn't hurry them. If you put them in a very warm, darkish place, you will soon find them bristling with long tender white shoots which all get broken off as soon as you handle them: that does more harm than good. What you want are those stocky little green sprouts which grow slowly, and are only about half an inch long at planting time, and not easily broken off. There are a good many eyes on a potato tuber, and they are all capable of growing out into a shoot, but you mustn't let them. All you want are two nice strong ones at the top of each tuber; if any more appear rub them off as soon as you see them. You will get a heavier crop of larger potatoes from two shoots, or even from one, than you will from half a dozen. Too many shoots mean too much crowded top growth, and a larger number of little potatoes. One strong shoot is really all that you need to produce a heavy crop; but I advise leaving two in case one gets accidentally broken. This is one of the real advantages of sprouting, it enables you to get a heavier crop and reduce the number of small potatoes, but remember, it must be done slowly, without any attempt at forcing, or if you are not careful you will have long thin sprouts long before it is time for planting. Occasionally in war-time seed potatoes are on the large size, and in the interests of economy a large tuber can be cut into two halves and these planted separately. But if you do cut them, don't do it on a dry windy day, and put the cut pieces out in the sun to dry, which at first sight looks the most sensible thing to do, but it isn't: the cut surface of a potato heals over quicker in a moist atmosphere. For my part, when I do any cutting I do it as I plant them, and put them straight into the ground. It usually answers very well, except in the case of Majestic, which is rather watery, and should never be cut at all. Majestic is an excellent potato, but it has that one fault, it is easily damaged. If you cut one in half now you will soon find beads of moisture oozing out of it, which you don't find in many other varieties. There is just one other point about cutting, always cut the tuber lengthwise, from top to bottom, not across, because you don't get such good results from the lower eyes as you do from the top ones; if there is one good sprout at the top end of each half it should be quite satisfactory. Let us be quite clear about this cutting business. I am not advising it as a matter of routine, and in the ordinary way I would rather not do it: the only advantage in it is that of economy and making the seed go further.

Next we come to the dates for planting. There are a good many old-fashioned ideas about planting potatoes. Some swear by Good Friday, others say Easter Monday and religiously plant the potatoes although it may be snowing or freezing. Personally I am no believer in gardening by specific dates; it is far better to consider the season, the weather and the condition of the soil. You cannot make any one rule for the whole country; on light soils, southern aspects, or sheltered gardens you can obviously plant much earlier than on heavy soils in cold districts. Generally speaking, I think we are all inclined to be in a hurry to plant potatoes. There is nothing gained by putting them into cold, stagnant soil, they will only be condemned to a miserable waiting period, and perhaps suffer considerably during the process. I always say don't plant until the spring sun has made its influence felt in the soil, and growth generally is active. If the potatoes are sprouted it doesn't hurt them to wait a week or two. I took part in some experiments once where we planted several varieties in

C *

early April. We planted a similar lot in early May and again in early June. We did this three years running. Two of the years the May planted batch gave the best results, and in the other one the June lot were the best. Admittedly this was on heavy land in the Midlands; on warmer land probably the April lot might have been better, but in our case they just hung fire and got frozen, while the others caught and passed them. Perhaps some of you were surprised, as I was, to hear Dr. Brett telling us a week or two ago that he didn't get his potatoes planted till early June, and yet got quite a good crop. That was undoubtedly an extreme case, and he might have had a better crop still if he had planted them in April. But it shows how difficult it is to rely on any particular time as being the best for planting. I have made a few observations in my time and have formed a few conclusions. In a general way I recommend the following approximate dates. For earlies, on light or medium soils, in the South and in warm areas, the first week in April; in the North or in cold exposed districts, and on heavy soils, the last week in April. For main-crops, a fortnight later in each case, except in warm districts where the soil is light, when I should plant them all together early in April. You can, of course, be too late on light soil, and, if you get a very dry period, growth may come to a stop before it has got into its stride. If, however, you are in any doubt about it, don't be afraid to wait a week, you will probably gain by doing so.

Then about the depth to plant. In a general way I should say in light soils the top of the tuber should be five inches below the surface, and in heavy soils, four

70

inches. Remember that the new potatoes are borne on stolons which spring from the stems above the planted tuber, so there should be a reasonable space between tuber and surface. On the other hand, the deeper you go the colder the soil, which means a slower start. The best way to plant potatoes is to chop out a trench with the spade and place the tubers, right way up, along the bottom of it, then cover them over. This is much better than using a dibber, which I call a lazy man's tool. It may be all right in crumbly dry soils, but in a sticky soil a dibber makes a deep hole, which as often as not gets full of water, with the potato stuck half-way down it. That doesn't give it much of a chance.

Distances are another controversial subject. More often than not we plant potatoes much too close together, and lose by it instead of gaining. I mentioned just now the heaviest crop I ever saw; they were planted eighteen inches apart in the rows, with the rows three feet apart. I'm afraid you would think it an awful waste of room to plant like that, but it usually pays, especially in the case of strong growers. I knew a man once who made a hobby of growing potatoes for exhibition. He never put them nearer than two feet apart in the rows, only allowed one stem to each plant, and tied them up to wires like tomato plants. I have seen them six feet high, and he used to lift extraordinary crops from them. Well, I'm not suggesting that to allotment holders, but I do suggest that you give them room; say, not less than two feet by one foot for the earlies, and not less than fifteen inches by two feet six for the others—a little more rather than a little less.

January

GARDEN AND GREENHOUSE

I SHALL be glad when this miserable war is over, so that I can talk about rock gardens and roses and lawns again, but for the moment it seems almost unpatriotic to think about such things. However, it so happens that I have had quite a lot of letters lately about lawns. That little patch of grass which is left to us seems to have become more precious than ever, and I am frequently being asked what sort of treatment to give it during the winter, so as to have it nice and green during the summer. Well, I can tell you that in a very few words. Don't roll it with a heavy roller, it makes the ground as hard as concrete, especially if the soil is at all heavy, and usually does more harm than good. Most garden books tell you in the autumn to clean up and oil the mowing machine and put it away for the winter. I don't know whether I'm a little contrary, but I never give that advice. I would rather clean up the roller and put that away for the winter, but keep the mower handy. A lawn is made up of a mixture of different kinds of grasses, some strong growing and very hardy, others finer and not so hardy. During mild periods in the winter the strong ones continue to grow, and often form coarse tufts which choke the finer grasses underneath and around them. So it is a good plan to run the mower over them occasionally, with the blades set high, and without the box, just to keep these coarser grasses within respectable limits. But don't use a mower or anything else on a lawn during frosty weather, and if there is snow on the grass, leave it there, don't sweep it off, it does the grass good. There is no point in feeding a lawn at this time of year, March is the time to think about that.

Talking of rockeries reminds me of an interesting suggestion which comes from a listener, and might appeal to some of you. Many of our principal cities and towns have been badly knocked about lately by Goering and Co., churches, hospitals and historical buildings have been destroyed or damaged. Now, the suggestion is that suitable stones should be selected from these buildings, marked in some way, and used to build a rock garden in the public park, which could be suitably planted and looked after, and become a permanent memorial to those who suffered during the air raids. What do you think of the idea? It seems rather a nice one to me, and I don't see that it would present any great difficulty. Not many of our parks can boast a rock garden, and this seems to present a golden opportunity of combining sentiment with beauty. It seems well worth thinking over. We are bound to have memorials springing up all over the country after the war, and, whatever form they take, it would surely be fitting to have them constructed with the actual stones from buildings which were destroyed, especially sacred or historic buildings, and to have growing flowers always associated with them would be the best of all. I should rather like the job of designing and building such a rockery.

But perhaps we had better get back to the kitchen front, which is the more important business of the moment. Once or twice lately, I have suggested the desirability of sowing certain vegetables under glass,

73

especially onions, and planting the little onions out of doors in May. This, as I have already pointed out, would mean a tremendous saving of seed, and would most likely result in earlier and better crops. Now I am receiving quite a number of letters on the subject, mostly from listeners who possess a nice little greenhouse, and have so far grown very little in it except tomatoes and a few flowers, and they all want to know how to raise onions and other vegetables. There is nothing very difficult about it, provided you can keep a temperature in the house of about 50° Fahrenheit. There is no need for excessive heat, indeed it does far more harm than good, and I daresay there are more failures due to keeping things too warm than to not having them warm enough. In the spring, when the seedling onions and other vegetables are coming up out of doors, the temperature is usually round about 50°, rising on warm days perhaps as high as 60°, but not often higher, and sometimes the nights are quite cold, as low as 40°, or lower. So we should try to produce these spring conditions under glass. We can't quite do it, because we are short of sunshine, but you can't make up for the lack of sunshine by giving extra warmth. You can vary between 45° and 55° with safety, and even up to 60° during a mild day, but that's quite enough, and if the house feels warm and dry, open the ventilators a little to cool it down.

The best way to sow onions is in flat seed trays or boxes. Suitable soil is a good ordinary garden loam, or old potting soil, with a fair amount of sand mixed with it, but no manure or leaf mould. A little fine peat mixed with it is quite good, it provides humus and helps to hold moisture, but strong manure is inclined to encourage fungus growth and cause the seedlings to damp off, besides they don't want manure in their early stages—that comes later on. The only fertiliser I use is a little superphosphate, one ounce well mixed with each bushel of soil—a bushel is about half a hundredweight. Superphosphate is excellent stuff for seeds, they seem to germinate much more freely and evenly when there is a little there, and get a better start. Before filling the boxes, it is best to sift the soil, putting the coarse stuff at the bottom for drainage, and topping up with the finer soil. Press it fairly firm with the fingers and give it a soaking with water and let it drain. Then sow the seed thinly and evenly over the surface, with the seeds all separated from each other if you possibly can. Then, if you've got a fine sieve, sift a little fine sandy soil over the seed, just enough to cover it, and press it down a little with a flat piece of wood. Finally, put a pane of glass over the box, with a little chip or something under one side for ventilation. As soon as the seeds have germinated, take the glass off, and keep the box on the greenhouse stage away from draughts, and where it can get as much daylight as possible. The pane of glass on the box is not absolutely necessary, but it seems to hurry up the germination. If the boxes get dry the best way to water is to hold them in a tank of water and allow it to percolate up from below till the surface is damp. This is better than pouring water over the boxes.

I'm afraid that seems rather a lot of detail, but it's the details that matter in these jobs. Don't leave the seedlings in the box till they are crowded together and starving, even if you have to transplant them twice into other boxes. It pays to keep them growing without checks or delays. When you transplant onions, whether in boxes or out of doors, keep them as shallow as you can. So long as the roots are underground and they will stand upright, the more there is out of the ground the better. Leeks you can plant as deep as you like, but not onions; if you plant them deeply they will have thick necks and perhaps look more like leeks than onions.

What else can we sow under glass beside onions? You can have a box of leeks; by getting them sown early they get a long season of growth and grow into good big ones for next winter or spring. You might try a box of lettuces, May Queen is a good variety for sowing and planting out early, but one box is usually enough, you don't want to get too many all at once. Celery is usually sown under glass, but next month would do for that. In fact, there are not many things, apart from onions, that need be sown till the middle of next month, except perhaps tomatoes. You will probably fill the house with tomatoes after the boxes have all been cleared out, and I expect you'll plant some out of doors as well, so if you are going to raise your own you can sow the seed as soon as you like, but don't forget that tomatoes like fresh air. If you keep them shut up close and warm you'll have them damping off as sure as eggs are eggs. And whatever you do, don't let them get overcrowded. The best plan is to pot them off singly into little pots when they are big enough to handle, and let them come along gently till the spring. Another useful vegetable which pays for early sowing is New Zealand spinach. When I say early I don't mean now.

Late next month or early March would do, and the simplest way is to sow them in small pots, one seed in a pot, and bring them on ready for planting out in May. New Zealand spinach is not nearly so widely grown as it ought to be, considering how popular spinach has become lately. The New Zealand kind grows and spreads about just like a nasturtium, and you can keep picking leaves and shoots from the same plants till well into the autumn. You might also sow a box of early cauliflowers. "All the Year Round" is a good variety, and by sowing now and planting out in the spring you can get some nice early ones. Some seeds are very difficult to see on the surface of the soil, and it is not easy to sow them thinly, especially if you are a beginner. It is quite a good plan to practise a little before you start sowing seriously. Lay a piece of rough white cloth or a dry towel on the table, and sprinkle the seeds over it with your thumb and first two fingers until you get the knack of sowing thinly and evenly. You'll be surprised how awkward you are at first, but after a few attempts you'll find it very much easier; but the easiest thing of all is to sow three or four times too much seed, and that is just what we mustn't do this year.

There are one or two things to remember when raising all seedling vegetables under glass. You can keep them a bit warm and close for the first week or two, but after that, while they are growing, they must have plenty of ventilation and all the light you can give them, otherwise they will grow up thin and weak, like children with the rickets, and then when you plant them out of doors it takes them a long time to get used to it. They ought to get gradually more and more fresh air, until they can be stood out of doors altogether, or in an open frame, for a week or two before planting out, except for a little protection on very cold nights. You must never give them sudden changes from warm conditions to cold. Another thing is the question of manure. Seedlings should start their life on a light diet without manure at all, except, as I said before about the onions, a pinch of superphosphate. Then transplant to something a little richer as they grow, finally planting out in well-prepared soil with something good in it. The worst thing to do is to bring seedlings on in rich soil, which only makes them grow soft, and then plant them out of doors in a poorer soil. That is doing it the wrong way round.

If you haven't got a greenhouse or frame, why not invest in a set of what are known as continuous cloches? These are little structures of glass and wire which fit over the rows of seedlings sown out of doors and bring them on much earlier as well as protecting them from enemies. It is surprising how quickly and well early vegetables and salads grow under these cloches, and when you've finished with them you can pack them away in a very small space. You often see them advertised in the garden press, and they are a sound investment.

Meanwhile, get that onion bed ready by digging it as deeply as you possibly can and mixing a barrow load or two of good farmyard manure or the remains of the compost heap with the lower soil. If you can't get these things invest in a bag of hop manure, poultry manure, or fish manure. We always advocate deep cultivation for onions (not deep planting) because they send their roots right down as the season advances. The roots of onions don't branch about like most other roots, they are rather like long strings, and I have traced them down as far as six feet below the surface, and so long as there is anything down below for them to find they will go down after it. We must do the best we can for the onions this year, and grow as many as we can, because they are going to be one of the most important crops in the garden.

February

METHOD IN SOWING AND PLANTING

I HOPE by this time you have got your cropping plans all ready, and know just where you are going to put everything when sowing and planting time comes. I have my doubts about it, though, because when visiting one or two friends lately I find that although they are full of enthusiasm they are very hazy about the details as to where the different crops are going, and how much of each they are likely to want. Some of my friends haven't begun to think about the garden yet; I suppose that is understandable, there isn't much in a vegetable garden at the present moment to create enthusiasm; the sight of a batch of wet shivering kales or spent brussels sprouts and frozen parsnips doesn't exactly spur the beginner on to great deeds, or fill him with the desire to be up and doing, so the work gets put off till a bit later on. But presently, and it won't be long, the crocuses will be blooming, the yew trees dusty with pollen, the sun shining and the birds singing, and then the gardening fever comes on us with a rush and a terrific onslaught begins. Many enthusiastic beginners start off in a great hurry to dig the ground, and as soon as they've got a bit ready, out come the seed packets and the excitement begins. In goes a row of peas, a couple of rows of spring carrots and some broad beans; then a bit more ground has to be dug. What goes in next? Oh yes, parsnips. They have to be sown early, so down go two or three rows; then some spinach and lettuce and a few rows of first early potatoes, and so the work goes on, rather hurriedly, and not too well done, because he finds he is getting a bit behind-hand with some of the things. In due course the summer comes, the peas are ready and used up, so are the broad beans and carrots and early potatoes and things, and then the beginner looks at his plot, scratches his head and says, "What a nuisance these three rows of parsnips are. I wish I'd put them somewhere else, up the other end, then I could have cleared this piece ready for the winter greens, but parsnips can't be moved, so I'm afraid they'll have to stop there now." The wise gardener doesn't do it that way, he has everything planned out in advance, puts all his early vegetables together and his late ones to themselves on another plot, so that the different sections of ground can be cleared conveniently and prepared for the following crop. I'm afraid I have told you this so many times that you must be tired of hearing it, but it is so essential that I make no apology for repeating it. Devote an evening or two now to working out a detailed plan of your garden, so that you know exactly where everything is to go, and it will save you any amount of time and trouble later on. We are getting plenty of opportunity just now to take note of the different vegetables we are eating every day, and to make up our minds to get a good supply next year of those we like best or find most profitable. Tastes are not all alike, and it wouldn't do for us all to want exactly the same things. Take swedes, for instance. Many people turn up their noses at them and won't eat them, so there isn't much point in growing them. Personally I like a dish of mashed swedes, and I'm inclined to grow a few more rather than less, because they have the great merit of being available all through the winter, and like parsnips, you can have a dish when you fancy them. The other morning I had a slice of swede fried with a rasher of bacon; it had been previously boiled, of course, and was left over from the day before. I wondered what I'd got at first and poked it about with my knife and fork, then I tasted it, found it very good indeed, and have had more since. I have also had beetroot fried in the same way. I daresay it sounds rather horrible to some of you, but try it before you pass judgment. Another vegetable we have been enjoying lately is the vegetable marrow. We allowed some to get ripe and hung them up in the kitchen, and now chop one up occasionally and cook it. The thick yellow buttery flesh of a ripe marrow is to my mind infinitely better flavoured and far more nutritious than the young marrow eaten in the summer, which is really unripe fruit. If you can get one try it, and by way of variety boil a little mint or other flavouring with it. It seems to me that in war-time at least, we ought to regard the marrow as a winter vegetable rather than a summer one. There are plenty of other things in the summer, and in making our plans at the present time we should keep next winter and early spring in our minds rather than the summer and autumn; we are not likely to go short of vegetables then. I sometimes feel half inclined to devote the whole garden to winter vegetables. I can get plenty of stuff in the summer and autumn from the neighbours, they usually want to give it to me, but I suppose it wouldn't do to rely on it. What other winter vegetables are you planning to grow? Potatoes, of course, and parsnips, carrots and beetroots. They are included as a matter of course. What about a row of Jerusalem artichokes? I asked a lady the other day if she liked artichokes, and she said, "I can't remember that I've ever tasted them." Would you believe it? A country woman too! We had a dish of them recently, there were five of us; four of us thoroughly enjoyed them, and the other, a Londoner, by the way, got one in his mouth and promptly spat it out again —thought he'd got hold of a lump of soap or something equally horrible, which just shows how tastes differ. But if you like artichokes, they are about the easiest of all vegetables to grow. You merely put the tubers in the ground in the spring, about six inches deep and a foot apart, and forget them till it's time to dig them up. They are very very handy for making a screen across the end of a plot, or for keeping the compost heap out of sight, and they don't have any diseases or bugs to look out for. Spinach beet is a good vegetable, if you like spinach, but you needn't sow that till the summer, after you have cleared off an early crop. Onions and shallots, of course. You've heard a good deal about them lately, and many of you know what it means to be without them, so I needn't advise you to grow more. Grow more leeks too, and get them sown early; if you can get them sown indoors now so much the better. The more time they get the bigger they grow, and if you've got a bed of good fat ones next winter you'll find them very useful. And what about an extra row of peas, not for eating in the summer, but for harvesting and drying for winter use? Peas are very wholesome. You merely let them get ripe, shell them and keep them dry, and during the winter you soak them and boil them, and make peas pudding with them if you

83

like. They won't be green like those you buy, but they won't be any the worse for that. And don't forget to make provision for kales and purple sprouting broccoli. Someone told me recently that I had purple sprouting broccoli on the brain; perhaps I have, but I guarantee you wouldn't turn up your nose at a nice dish of it next March, when there is no other green vegetable to be had. And now suppose we switch over for a minute or two to the flower garden.

Walking across the garden the other day I came across a bush of witch hazel in full flower; a lovely picture, rather like a bush covered with golden spiders shining in the pale sunlight, and close by was a little Daphne bush, with its first pink flowers beginning to open. The scent from the witch hazel was delightful; it filled the cold air for yards around, and as I stood and sniffed at it I almost forgot the Dig for Victory campaign for the moment, and allowed my thoughts to wander back to the glories of our pre-war flower gardens. Won't it be grand when we can have them back again, when we can sit on the old garden seat once more on a summer evening with scented lilies, stocks and sweet peas all around us, and listen to the birds instead of the sirens? May it come soon! For the moment, however, the garden seat is upside down behind the wood shed, the few rose bushes, forsythias and flowering currants which survived the great autumn purge, are huddled together in a far corner, wondering what they have done to deserve it all, and the order of the garden now is food, and ever more food—munitions of war. But we must have a few flowers too ; life would be altogether too dull and depressing without them. So while we are planning and scheming to get the maximum of food from the vegetable garden and allotment, let us try to include a few flowers in the scheme as far as is possible without interfering with the more essential side of the business. Those little front gardens, for instance. Nearly every house has one, and it isn't of much use for growing vegetables, so why not make it as bright and colourful as possible, to cheer up, not only ourselves, but others who pass by? I passed by a good many last year, and most of them were rather drab and dreary affairs. Perhaps a privet hedge and a grass patch by the side of a path, or a depressing evergreen tree overshadowing everything. Here and there one found a cheerful, well-kept little garden, which shone like a jewel in a bad setting. The point is that practically none of these little front gardens was producing an ounce of food, and they are not very likely to do so even this year, so they might just as well be producing flowers. Some of them are doing so, of course, and doing it very nicely. I know one suburban avenue which last year set an example which many others might well follow. Nearly every front garden seemed full of colour. Most of them, instead of a forbidding looking front hedge, had a low, rough stone wall, so that the garden was open to view, and a few of them had even overflowed in front of the wall with a strip of rock work, bright with aubretias, pinks and other creeping plants, while the gardens themselves were full of annuals and other pretty flowers. I paid several visits to that avenue, and it struck me that from some of the gardens anyone could have gathered a bunch of roses and walked off with them, but I don't believe anyone ever did. Now, at first

85

sight it looked as though these people were a little unpatriotic, and ought to have devoted their energies to growing vegetables instead of flowers, but I soon had an opportunity of seeing the back gardens as well as the front, and in nearly every case I found that the back garden was well cropped with an abundant supply of vegetables. As the season passed I discovered that it was almost an invariable rule that where you found a bright, well-kept front garden, you also found a well-stocked vegetable garden at the back, but where you found a shabby front garden you nearly always found a shabby back garden too. Which is the better example to follow? I leave the answer to you.

Very well, then, let us think of a few nice front garden flowers to brighten up the summer months. We shall want something colourful which will last over as long a period as possible. The hybrid polyantha roses, such as Karen Poulsen, Else Poulsen, and the other Poulsens are very nice to colour up the space under the bay window; they flower freely from June till November, and their pink and red flowers are very attractive. The dwarf dahlias, of the Coltness Gem type, put up a good show too; planted in May a foot or eighteen inches apart they produce a mass of bright flowers all through the summer till the frost comes. Antirrhinums are good stayers too, and always attractive, especially in association with blue lobelia and white alyssum. I daresay you will be able to get boxes of these in the spring ready for planting out. The bedding petunias are very nice too, and have the additional charm of sweet scent in the evening. If you would rather do it with a few packets of seeds there are plenty to choose from. Marigolds are bright and attractive, so are nasturtiums, especially the Tom Thumb, or bedding varieties, which make nice compact plants covered with flowers all through the summer, and they will grow and flower well on poor soil where very few other flowers will grow. Scarlet flax, blue nemophila, godetias, annual rudbeckias, sweet scabious, cornflowers and coreopsis, with a few stocks and asters and scarlet salvias will keep up a show of colour over a long period, and there will be flowers to greet you every evening when you get home after a tiring day. And why not a bit of rockwork? You can get endless pleasure out of a heap of soil and a few well placed stones, planted with aubretias, campanulas, pinks, Alpine phloxes and other pretty little rock plants which you can buy in pots from any good nursery. And don't forget, if you want a spring show, that there is still time to plant wallflowers, forget-me-nots, polyanthuses and double daisies. I daresay all this sounds very frivolous just now, but so long as you give first place to the vegetable crops and grow all you can, I, for one, can see no earthly reason why you shouldn't have your flowers as well, and personally I should like to see the small front gardens looking gayer with flowers this year than they have ever looked before. We should all feel better and more cheerful for it.

SPRING

March

SEEDS

IT is nice to think that another winter has passed away. It may linger a bit longer and give us a few more spiteful spasms, but nothing, not even war, can prevent the sun shining and the crocuses blooming. So let us roll up our sleeves and greet the spring with a smile, and a determined resolution to make this one of the biggest gardening years ever.

First, let us talk about sowing seeds, one of the most interesting of all gardening jobs. At least, it is to me. I always think of a seed as one of the wonders of the world. I have some in front of me now, tiny little things which might be a charge of duck shot; there is no sign of anything alive about them; you can cut one open and look at it through a magnifying glass, but you don't find much. You can have one chemically analysed, and that doesn't tell you much either. Yet each one of these little seeds contains the embryo of a living plant, and we know in advance what that plant is going to be. I have just examined three seeds which appear to be exactly alike in every respect. Yet, given ordinary conditions, one will produce a cauliflower plant, one a brussels sprout, and one a cabbage, with all the different characteristics and flavours of these plants.

This question of flavour always fascinates my simple mind. One variety of pea or bean or tomato has a nicer or different flavour from another. Why? What causes

88

the difference? You can graft one variety of apple on to another, so that half the tree bears sweet rosy dessert apples, and the other green sour ones. Yet they are both on the same roots, getting the same food from the soil, breathing the same air; what causes the difference? Some scientist might be able to explain it, but I'm bothered if I can.

We take all these things for granted, we accept seeds more or less as a matter of course; but it's nice to ponder over it sometimes and try to appreciate the wonders of these things and the convenience of them. Let us thank God for seeds, which seem to be sent specially for our benefit to enable us to keep a future garden of flowers and vegetables in a cupboard for the winter, and to send it safely to the four quarters of the globe. Gardening would be a difficult business without seeds. The germination of a seed, too, is something to marvel at. This dry dormant little thing only needs moisture, air and warmth to bring life to it again. The moisture penetrates the covering and the seed begins to swell, a tiny rootlet pushes its way out in one direction and the shoot or plantlet in another, and no matter which way up the seed is, the rootlet always turns down to the earth and the shoot upwards to the light. Meanwhile the hard substance of the seed is dissolved by warmth, air and moisture, and diluted into baby food, to feed the little shoot and the tiny root until it is able to fend for itself and take its nourishment from the soil, and so a new plant is born. The new roots absorb raw chemicals from the soil and pump them up through the plant, where the leaves, by some wonderful process aided by the sun and the air, convert those raw chemicals into sugar, starch and other good foods; which we in turn take from them to feed ourselves with.

Does it ever occur to you how dependent we poor humans are on growing plants and green leaves? All the food we eat comes from the raw materials in the soil, but we couldn't use them direct, and we couldn't convert them into food. Plants have to do that for us; they are cleverer than we are, they manufacture their own food, and ours too. Even when we eat meat we are eating the same sort of food second-hand, or more highly developed. It all came from the raw chemicals of the soil in the first place, through the roots and leaves of plants, which started their existence from one of these tiny seeds. So when you contemplate a seed, think of it as the source of your daily bread, and treat it with due respect.

There is another point about seeds which is of interest. A seed itself is filled with highly concentrated food, which, as I said before, is diluted down and slowly liberated to feed the infant plant during germination. That, presumably, is its primary function. But Nature is so lavish in the production of seeds that only a small percentage of them are needed to carry on the race. The bulk of them are produced for our benefit, and our most nourishing and cheapest food consists of surplus seeds, in the form of cereals, bread, peas, beans and so on, thanks to Nature's abundant gifts. We ought to think of these things sometimes and be duly grateful, and more especially for the fact that the Great Architect who designed this marvellous scheme, has given us, as gardeners, a measure of control over it, so that we can assist Nature to produce more and more of these valuable foods which keep us alive and well.

As gardeners we know something of the soil, what a treasure house it is, and what great gifts it has in store for us if we handle it wisely and well and make the most of our opportunities. Some people rarely give a thought to the soil, except to regard it as dirt, something unpleasant, to be avoided. Perhaps it is difficult to realise that it produces everything we possess. Your gold watch and jewellery, every house, motor-car, airplane, ship, guns, all came from the soil, thanks to the power given to us to extract them from it. The tragedy is that these great gifts should be used for the destruction of mankind, instead of for his benefit. I wonder if this, too, is part of the great scheme of life, a process of levelling and balancing? But perhaps I had better give up wondering, and get back to the garden and seed sowing.

If all the seeds which are produced in wild life grew into plants, they would choke each other, and life would be impossible; but they don't; only a very small percentage grow to maturity. The great majority are either eaten by birds and animals, or find themselves in unsuitable places, where the little roots can find neither anchorage nor food, and so they perish. But in our gardens we want them all, or at least the majority, to germinate and grow, so we produce suitable conditions for them to do so, by forking and raking down the surface soil till it is fine and soft—what gardeners call a good tilth—so that the seeds will be in contact with the moist soil, and at the same time air and warmth can penetrate.

Some soils are inclined to cake and form a crust on the surface which makes it very uncomfortable for seedlings. I find that a good way to avoid this is to spread a little fine peat over the soil, say half a pound to a square yard, and rake it well into the surface. You can buy this peat from most nurseries, or a little of the peat moss litter as used in stables would do quite well. It keeps the soil open and prevents caking, and it also helps to hold moisture, which is very necessary for seeds. Another thing which seedlings like is a phosphate, either superphosphate or steamed bone flour are good; they have a direct influence on new root systems, and nearly all seedlings respond to it, and germinate and establish themselves much better when it is present. You don't need much, one ounce to a square yard raked into the soil before sowing is enough, but it does make a difference. I use superphosphate, and I always mix a little with the soil when I sow seeds in pots and boxes. Apart from that, seeds don't need manure, especially on a seed-bed, where they only remain a short time; they are better without it during infancy.

If you are sowing seeds where they have got to remain and grow, then it's best, if you can, to prepare the ground with the manure about six inches below the surface, so that the seedlings have built up a good root system before they reach it, then they can take it. We usually sow seeds by drawing out drills or shallow trenches with the hoe, dribbling the seeds along them, and then raking the soil over them.

Some people find it difficult to distribute small seeds evenly, and use tins with holes in, or sugar dredgers or similar gadgets, but I don't think such things are really necessary; others mix the seed with sand before sowing, and get a better distribution that way. But I think with a little practice it isn't difficult to sow them evenly. For my part, I merely empty the packet into the palm of my left hand and then take pinches with my right finger and thumb, or rather two fingers and thumb, and scatter them thinly along the drill. Of course, you have to bend your back. You can't stand upright and drop them, your right hand should be almost touching the ground.

The easiest mistake of all is to sow them far too thickly, especially small seeds, which are usually dark in colour, and difficult to see on the soil. You must try to avoid that, because the more you sow, the more you will have to pull out and waste. In the case of large seeds like peas and beans it is better to place the seeds in one at a time, properly spaced out, it doesn't take much longer, and it gives better results.

The width of a drill is also important, and varies according to the crop. For peas, for instance, you can make a drill as much as six inches wide, and distribute the seeds evenly across it, but for small seeds like lettuce, spinach and cabbages on the seed-bed, narrow drills are better, to enable the hoe to operate safely between the rows.

Anything which has to be thinned out to specified distances, such as beet, turnips and so on, is better sown in a straight thin line; but short carrots can be sown thinly in a wider drill, say three inches, and then left unthinned till the biggest are ready for use. You dodge the fly a bit that way, because the carrots are not disturbed so much, and it is when you handle them that the smell is given off which attracts the fly. Onions can be grown like that too without any thinning, but you have to be mighty careful to sow the seed sparingly,

D

or else they will come up too crowded and spoil each other. Of course that won't do if you want big onions and carrots, they have to be properly spaced out, but I have had many a crop of good serviceable onions without any thinning at all.

Depth is another point to be considered, it should vary according to the size of the seed. Peas and beans can be a good inch deep, but very small seeds need hardly be covered at all. Some of the smallest flower seeds are merely scattered over the surface and raked in, but most vegetable seeds are better covered over with at least a little soil, but you can easily put them in too deeply. As the summer advances, the soil gets warmer and drier, so the later you sow the deeper the seeds should be. The peas you are sowing now, for instance, needn't be more than half an inch deep, but those you sow in June can be down one and a half inches, where they are not so likely to get dry during their infancy.

While we are on the subject of seeds, I might mention that I am often told of the difficulties some people have in getting seeds of hardy Alpine plants to germinate. I think it is very often due to the fact that those seeds are kept through the winter in warm dry cupboards, where they get thoroughly hard and spoilt. In their native country they would merely drop on to the ground, and remain there under the snow all the winter. I have found that if you leave these seeds in boxes of soil out of doors all the winter, they germinate quite well when the spring arrives.

Finally, just a word about transplanting seedling vegetables. It is, of course, a great convenience to be able to do this. It enables us to arrange our cropping much more effectively, and get more out of the garden. But from the plants' point of view, transplanting is by no means a necessity. Nearly all vegetables are better if they can grow from seed to maturity without being disturbed. It is difficult, almost impossible, to move a plant without tearing off its tiny little delicate feeding roots, and this gives it a check from which it has to recover. Don't transplant if it isn't necessary, and when you do, handle the plant as carefully as possible, and before its roots get badly tangled up with the next one. Don't let seedlings get crowded together so that you have to tear them apart, it hurts them.

April

WAR-TIME FLOWERS

ALTHOUGH I hope we are all going to make stupendous efforts this year to increase the supply of home-grown food, I also hope that every garden is going to find room for a few flowers, because I think the cheerful company of brightly coloured flowers is more necessary now than ever.

Naturally our floral efforts will be a good deal less ambitious than they are in normal times, and most of us will have less space to devote to them, but that is all the more reason why we should choose carefully, and make up in quality what we lack in quantity. As this is the seed-sowing season, I particularly want to talk about annuals to-day, which are so easily grown from seeds, and provide a means of getting a good show of bright flowers with a minimum of cost and attention.

The cultivation of hardy annuals is simplicity itself; indeed, I think failures are more often due to over-kindness and coddling than to neglect. Before the war it was becoming fashionable to devote entire borders to annuals, borders of patchwork colour all grown from packets of seed sown on the spot, and very cheerful they were too. I'm afraid we can't afford whole borders of them this year, but we can all find odd corners and spaces which are simply asking to be filled with a few bright flowers. Before sowing, which is usually early next month, the soil should be dug over with the fork, and if you can spare a little good manure so much the better, but get it well down below the surface so that the seedlings don't find it too soon, otherwise they will grow too fat and tender, and flop all over the place. You can easily make soil too rich for annuals, and get all leaves and growth and very few flowers. On the other hand, if the soil is too poor, they start flowering before they've had a chance to grow into decent plants. So we want to avoid extremes and find the happy medium, a soil neither too poor nor too rich. I find a little fine bonemeal raked into the soil before sowing is one of the best things to give them a good start, about two ounces to a square yard, it makes quite a big difference. Make the surface soil nice and fine with the rake, and then sow the seeds by simply scattering them sparingly over the soil, and raking them in. In the case of some of the larger seeds, such as annual lupins, you can shake a little soil over them through a sieve, but for most of the small seeds the rake is all that is necessary. Mind you don't sow them too thickly, you nearly always do, and then you have to pull most of them out again, and drastic thinning always goes against the grain, especially with beginners. Hardy annuals, as a rule, don't like to be transplanted, that is why we usually sow them where they are to remain, and thin out the surplus ones; and thin them out early, before the roots get tangled together. Weeds are the worst enemies of annuals, if you allow them to grow in competition with them, so you mustn't. You must pull them out as soon as you see them, and mind you don't pull your annuals out and leave the weeds. Some of the weeds are better looking in their early stages than some of the annuals and sometimes they are very much alike, so it is not difficult to make that mistake until you get to know them well. When the annuals are up, and thinned out, a few short branching twigs stuck among them will keep them upright, and, with a few exceptions, that is all the staking they require. The only subsequent attention necessary is to keep the faded flowers picked off to prevent seed-pods forming. A plant soon stops flowering if it is allowed to carry seed-pods.

There are many nice annuals to choose from: far more than most of us can accommodate in the war-time border, so we may as well select a few of the best, preferably those with bright colours, not too tall or spreading, and which last in flower over a reasonably long period.

Let us think of a few! I will start with a very common one, eschscholtzia, which some gardeners treat with as much respect as they would chickweed, and certainly some of the old kinds of eschscholtzias, which often resembled inverted spring carrots, were nothing very great. But some of the newer ones are different altogether. There are doubles as well as singles, and you can get named varieties, such as Flambeau, Carmine King, and Crimson Glow, in the most brilliant shades of crimson and orange. Try a few of the new ones and see for yourself. We will pass over marigolds, not because I don't want to include them, I do, but I've said enough about them in the past, and you all know them, although you may not all know the new varieties, they are worth looking up. A pretty little flower which is just right for small spaces is the linaria; it produces small spikes of flowers something like tiny antirrhinums, and in almost every colour of the rainbow. Linaria fairy bouquet, is a delightful mixture, and most seedsmen sell it; if you sow the seed sparingly, you needn't do much thinning afterwards, but you won't find it easy to sow sparingly, the seed is so small.

Nasturtiums are good war-time flowers, because they put up a brave show of colour, and seem to thrive on a poor diet. In a rich soil they produce too many leaves, and the flowers are hidden among them. There was a remarkable example of this at the Wisley Gardens last summer. At intervals along a broad border of annuals are flowering crabs and other ornamental trees, and surrounding these, and right up to the main stem, dwarf nasturtiums were planted. Under the trees, and out as far as the spread of the branches they made a perfect carpet of brilliant colour, but those outside the influence of the tree grew much larger and formed a kind of heavy green ring around the bed of colour. It wasn't a question of shade, the trees are young standards, and the nasturtiums got plenty of sunshine, but in competition with the tree roots they grew less vigorously and flowered much more freely. The moral is, don't be too kind to nasturtiums; treat them rough and half starve them and they flower all the better for it. We used to deplore the wandering habits of nasturtiums, and only plant them where they had plenty of room to sprawl, but many of the modern dwarf varieties, such as Rosy Morn and Fireball, make bushy compact little plants, and hold the flowers well above the foliage, which makes them ideal for borders or for covering bare banks. I ought to remind you, of course, that nasturtiums are not hardy, and shouldn't be sown till the end of April or early May, and they should be spaced out about nine inches apart. Shirley poppies are dainty flowers, every year brings new colours and forms, doubles as well as singles; their soft art shades and silky petals are really lovely, especially when you get a close-up view of them in the morning sunlight. I always think if you want to see the full beauty of annuals you must get up early in the morning, when the petals are fresh and glistening in the slanting rays of the sun. They are inclined to look a bit jaded, as if they were suffering from a hangover, in the midday sun. On the other hand, if you want to get the full glory of the scented kinds you must visit them after the sun has gone down. You would never know that some of them were scented at all if you only saw them in the hours of sunshine. Mignonette, sweet alyssum, night scented stock, verbenas, tobacco flowers and even antirrhinums all give off their sweetest fragrance during the hours of darkness; they seem to spend the night making themselves up, so that they can present their fullest beauty to the rising sun. Nearly all our summer flowers are more or less scented, some very subtle and elusive, and some so bashful about it that they keep it a secret until we are all in bed, and only share it with the night-flying moths; but it is there all the same, and is often worth sitting up for.

But I was talking about Shirley poppies and their early morning beauty, which is worth getting up to see. Sow the seeds very thinly, and as they come up, thin them out to six inches apart, but don't try to transplant them; they won't have it. Nigella, commonly called love-in-the-mist, is a favourite flower of mine, it is such a lovely shade of blue, and perhaps more than most annuals it pays for a little kindly treatment. If you sow it on poor soil, especially in a dry sunny place all you get is a thin little stem with a tired looking grey-blue flower which suggests a headache. But sow it in good soil in semi-shade, and sow it early, before this month is out, and thin out the plants to six inches apart and it will grow into a pretty feathery plant and show you the real beauty of its flowers.

Another charming blue flower is *Phacelia viscida* (Musgrave strain); this has flowers about half an inch across, rather like bright blue buttercups, only wider open, and it grows and flowers freely over quite a long period, but not so long as I should like it to. It needs sowing again when the first batch is fading if you want to keep it with you all the summer. It is dwarf and bushy and likes about six inches of space. One of the brightest of annuals is the so-called scarlet flax (*Linum Grandiflora rubrum*); it bears masses of vermilion flowers about the size of half-pennies, its growth is rather weedy, and if you start handling it and try to thin it out, it is inclined to flop about and get its hair out of curl. The better way is to sow the seed very thinly and then leave it alone. Last year I sowed a patch of this linum with *Phacelia viscida* on one side and coreopsis " dazzler" on the other, and when they were all in flower they made a brave splash of colour. Next to the coreopsis I sowed some pale blue viscaria, which also played a noble part in the colour scheme. Coreopsis "dazzler" is a dwarf, compact variety, it grows about a foot high, and produces masses of yellow and chocolate flowers, prettily marked; it is better if thinned out to at least six inches. Some people use the name coreopsis, and some calliopsis. I'm not going to argue about it. I believe, strictly speaking, the perennial kinds are coreopsis, and the annuals

D *

calliopsis, but I call them all coreopsis; in any case the flowers are just as lovely under either name.

If you like the yellow and bronze coloured flowers, sow a patch of the newer annual rudbeckias. You all know the tall-growing perennial kinds, such as the "cone flower," but you mustn't confuse these with the annuals. These are quite small-growing plants, and they produce yellow and bronze, single and double flowers, mostly on stiff stems which make them ideal for cutting. There are several of them, with attractive names like "Golden Sunset" and "Autumn Glow," some are clear yellow, and others have reddish-brown rings in the flowers.

Godetias are old-fashioned flowers which have been, shall we say, improved out of all recognition; some of the recent additions are very suitable for a small border because they make dwarf, compact plants which are simply a mass of flowers, and in quite a wide range of unusual colours, both double and single flowers. Look up a good catalogue, and you will find quite a number of varieties to choose from. If you didn't think much of godetias when you were boys and girls, try them again now and note the difference. Finally, here is a dainty little annual specially recommended for those who keep bees, its name is *Linnanthes Douglasii*. It is very dwarf, suitable either for the rockery or the front of a border, and it produces masses of yellow and white flowers, which are a very happy and, I believe, profitable hunting ground for the bees.

the turf off and stack it out of the way, instead of burying it, as we advised in the autumn; the grass may refuse to melt now, and would perhaps be a nuisance during the summer. First job after digging, sprinkle a little finely powdered lime over the soil; a quarter of a pound to a square yard, and also some fine bonemeal, at two ounces to the square yard. Dried blood is another good fertiliser for new ground, one ounce to a square yard. Fork these into the surface soil and break it down as finely as you can ready for seed sowing, and the sooner you get busy with the seed packets now the better. There is no hurry for potato planting, except for a couple of rows of first earlies, such as Duke of York, or Sharpe's Express. The main crop can wait for another fortnight or three weeks. Plant the earlies in rows at least two feet apart, and one foot between the tubers in the rows. The best way is to plant them in trenches with a spade, with the top of the potatoes four inches below the surface. Perhaps the first of the small seeds to be sown now are the parsnips. You are already about a month late with them, but never mind that, better late than never. There is still time. The easiest way is to make narrow little trenches or drills with the hoe, an inch deep and a foot apart, and drop the seeds along it at nine-inch intervals, two or three in each place and rake the soil over them. When they come up thin them out to one in each place. Put these right at the end of the plot, so that they don't get mixed up with the early vegetables. At that end you will also put your celery trench, late potatoes, runner beans, and other late crops, so as to keep the lates together and the earlies together. At the other end you can start with a row of peas.

Gradus and Pilot are good varieties for beginners, they grow about three feet high, and need staking, but they are well worth the trouble. If you don't want the bother of staking you can sow a row of dwarfs, such as English Wonder or Little Marvel. You don't get the weight of crop with these, but they are nice little peas, and don't need staking. All the same, even these are all the better for a few short sticks, to keep them off the ground.

If you can possibly get a bundle of boughs, take my tip and grow a row of tall ones, they look better, crop better, and the peas are better. If you are particularly fond of broad beans, put a double row across the plot, with the beans six inches apart each way and two inches deep. I'm afraid the autumn and early spring sown broad beans have gone west, victims of Jack Frost, so most people have had to sow again, if they want any. It just shows what a frost it was, to kill the broad beans, and even the greens; it even killed the magnificent mimosa tree which was such a popular feature at the Wisley Gardens, and all the lovely genaothuses on the walls there are as dead as mutton. I hope it will be a long, long time before we see another winter like it. But perhaps we had better forget it, and stick to the allotment.

Next I suggest a row of spinach, the round seeded or true spinach; most people like spinach, it's supposed to be very good for you, there's a lot of iron and vitamins and minerals and things in it, so even if you don't like it, you had better eat it, it's as good as a dose of medicine for you.

By the way, have you ever eaten stinging nettles. When I was a youngster my mother used to gather and boil the young nettles in the spring and make us eat them for dinner. We used to call it mock spinach, and as far as I can remember the flavour was something like turnip tops. Boiling took the sting out of the young leaves, and they were not at all bad. I have even heard people say they were delicious. I wouldn't go so far as that, but they were supposed to prevent us getting spots on our noses or something, and they certainly did no harm. I've eaten a good many in my time, but perhaps that's no recommendation. It reminds me of a story of a little girl who wouldn't let Grandma wash her face before going to bed, and Grandma said, "Oh, but you must, when I was a little girl like you I always washed my face."

"Yes," said the little girl, "and now look at it."

Anyway, if you're hard up for spring greens, try a boiling of very young nettle tops, you needn't eat them if you don't like them. Call them Egyptian spinach, and see what the family has to say. Meanwhile I'm going to try a dish on Freddie Grisewood, and later on we'll compare notes.

Summer spinach is easy and quick to grow, provided the soil is deep and moist. On dry, shallow soil it runs to seed too quickly. You merely dribble the seeds along a drill nearly an inch deep, and rake the soil over them. Cut it and use it when it's about nine inches high, before it gets old and tough. There's another kind of spinach called spinach beet which is excellent for allotments. It's really a form of green-leaved beetroot, and you sow the seeds in drills an inch deep, and when they come up, thin them out to six inches apart. Then you keep pulling off the outer leaves for cooking as spinach, and more grow to take their places. I mention this now, but it isn't time to sow it yet. You don't really need it in the summer, so it's best to wait and sow a couple of rows a foot apart in the middle of summer, say July, then it will last you on and off all through next winter, provided next winter is a bit more respectable than the last one.

Of course you'll want a row of runner beans, no allotment is complete without them. It isn't time to sow them yet, but you had better reserve a space for them on the late plot. Right at the end of the allotment is as good a place as anywhere. Last year a friend of mine grew his runners in the form of a square, or at least three sides of a square, and in the space formed by them he had his compost heap. He also kept his barrow there, and on a warm day you could usually find him sitting in the barrow, either smoking his pipe or just asleep in the shade of the beans.

However, when you've decided where to put them, get the soil ready by digging out a trench, eighteen inches wide, and as deep as you conveniently can. Put all the dead leaves you can find along the bottom of the trench, and any old worn-out woollen socks you may have; cover them with a layer of soil, and then a layer of farm manure if you can get it. If not, a bag of hop manure will be a good substitute. Fill up the trench and leave it to settle. Then on the first of May, or thereabout, sow the beans, two inches deep and nine inches apart in a double row, and give them some good strong poles to climb up. You can get a row of beans without doing all this, but you'll get a much better one if you do.

At the early end of the plot sow two rows of carrots, the short horn or stump-rooted varieties. Sow the seed very thinly in drills half an inch deep, then let them grow without thinning till the biggest are about the size of your thumb or a good-sized walnut, and start pulling the big ones out for use. Carrots are delightful when pulled fresh and young like this (very tasty, very sweet), and if you sow a few, say a couple of rows, at fortnightly intervals, till August Bank holiday, you can keep up the supply till Christmas. If you want a crop of the big kinds for the winter store, don't sow them till June, then they are not so likely to be attacked by fly, and won't get coarse and split. Try a few rows of onions; some people say onions are difficult to grow and gardeners make a tremendous fuss of them, but they are usually out for great big ones, which are not necessary for our purpose. Admittedly onions like the deepest and richest soil you can give them, so if you can get a couple of barrow loads of good muck under them, so much the better, but if you do, get it buried well below the surface. If you can't get that, give the soil a dressing of bonemeal at the rate of two ounces to a square yard. Another excellent food for onions is ground hoof. Goodness knows where they find all the hoofs to grind up, or whether they are horses' hoofs, or the cloven hoofs of all the devils which have been let loose lately, but there seems to be a fair supply of it about, and most dealers sell it. Sprinkle it over the soil at the rate of two ounces per square yard, and get it well raked in. Raking is important when you are preparing an onion bed, you want the surface soil as fine as you can get it, but before the final raking you should tread it down, if it isn't too sticky or heavy, so that you finish with two inches of fine soil overlying a fairly firm under soil.

Then sow your seed in narrow drills, half an inch deep, rake them over well, walk along the rows to press the seeds and soil together, and finish with another light raking to leave a neat finish. If you choose a reliable variety, such as Bedfordshire Champion, or James' Long Keeping, and sow the seed very sparingly and carefully, you needn't do any more thinning, but if they come up too thickly, you must thin them out to three or four inches apart. You won't get big onions this way, but are more likely to get a good crop of serviceable ones, which will be just as welcome in the kitchen. Which reminds me that the recipe I gave for cooking potatoes was very well received. I had quite a lot of letters about it, so here is one for onions. Select medium-sized onions, peel them and partly boil them, enough to soften them, but not enough to break them. Then put them upright in a baking tin, with a piece of dripping on the top of each onion, and square lumps of cheese between them. Bake in the oven till crisp and brown, serve with bread and butter, and open the window for the benefit of the neighbours. This is an excellent dish for flighty husbands; give it to them about twice a week and no other woman will go near them.

April

FILLING THE SALAD BOWL

I HOPE you are having a good time with the seed packets, and not wasting too much time watching to see if the things are coming up. One of the first things I want to talk about to-day is the salad bowl. We are all interested in food values just now, and later on we shall all be eating beans and carrots and potatoes, and getting as fat as pigs if we are not careful. So to balance the diet, and keep ourselves fit, we are told we must eat plenty of green leaves, and we must eat them raw, not cooked, because cooking destroys some of those mysterious substances called vitamins which we hear so much about. There are several of them, and by all accounts they are very necessary and important; they help to digest the other foods, keep your eyes bright and your complexion clear, and prevent your hair falling out. In fact, the vitamins do us more good and keep us in better health than a daily dose of medicine. Have you ever noticed that when a cat feels out of sorts it goes and eats grass? And soon gets better, which shows that it knows more about vitamins than I do—it wouldn't know much if it didn't. But I do know that they are an essential part of our daily diet, and I also know that nearly all of them are found in green leaves, especially lettuce leaves, so if you want to keep fit, eat plenty of lettuce, but to be able to do that you'll first have to grow them, or at least you ought to, so that those grown by the market gardeners can go to the unfortunate people who have no gardens or allotments. In this country we eat far more lettuces than we did twenty years ago; before the last war we grew more of the tall growing cos varieties, and very few of the cabbage types. The Belgian refugees started the taste and demand for them, and production has steadily increased ever since. One large lettuce grower told me that he sends every year, I think it was three hundred and sixty thousand crates of lettuces into the London markets alone. It seemed a staggering figure, so I said, " Good gracious, who eats 'em all?" or something equally brilliant, and he sharply reminded me that that quantity worked out at less than half a lettuce per head per annum for the population of London, and that they ought to eat twenty times the quantity, so if we are going to increase the consumption of lettuces, it seems pretty certain that there won't be enough to go round, especially as in normal times we import about £400,000 worth every year, so we had better set to and grow a few more ourselves.

The first thing to remember about lettuces, and indeed all salads, is that we want crisp tender leaves, which means that they must be grown quickly without checks or delays in good soil which does not get dry. You can't grow nice tender lettuces on shallow, dry soil in the hot baking sun. Apart from that, they are very accommodating, you can grow them among the other crops alongside the celery trench, or in any odd corner so long as there is some good soil there. Some gardeners can always cut a nice fresh lettuce during the summer, others have a grand lot for a week or so and then none, or a few old tough ones, with dead leaves to be removed, you know the sort I mean. That's because they sow too many at a time, and then can't eat them while they are at their best. The way to keep up a nice, steady supply is to make very small sowings, just a short row, about once a week from now till the middle of August. Suppose, after you've thinned them out or transplanted them, you get a dozen from each sowing, that should be plenty for two of you; very few people eat more than one lettuce a day, even if they are on diet, so there is no point in growing a lot. You can sow the seed sparingly in drills, half an inch deep, and thin them out when they come up to nine inches apart, or you can sow them on the seed-bed and transplant them when ready. Those which are not transplanted are usually ready a little quicker, but there isn't much in it, so long as you handle them gently when transplanting, and don't break them all to bits, and expect them to be none the worse for it. Give the soil a light dressing of a good general fertiliser, or a little dried blood or, better still, ground hoof if you can get it; lettuces like ground hoof, but don't overdo it, half an ounce to each yard of row, well raked in, is enough.

There are so many good varieties to choose from that I hesitate to mention any, but of the cabbage varieties, I like Trocadero, Continuity, and Commodore Nutt, and if you prefer the cos or tall varieties, I don't think you can go far wrong with Balloon Giant white, and Jumbo, they are both good lettuces, and give you plenty for your money, but there are plenty of other good varieties, and I daresay a local gardener could give you better advice on the subject than I can.

The main thing with lettuces, and all other salads, is not to let them get dry. I don't believe in watering vegetables as a rule, but salads are different, you can't get tender, juicy leaves if the roots are dry.

Another good salad you might bear in mind is endive, it makes a delightful salad to follow the lettuces in the autumn. There is no point in sowing it yet, June is early enough, but you may as well order a packet of seed of the curled type of endive, and perhaps we shall have an opportunity of discussing it again later on.

A salad which very few people grow is corn salad, or Lamb's lettuces. It is very easy to grow, you just sow a few seeds any time during the summer, either broadcast or in drills, and rake them in. If you sow them sparingly you can leave them unthinned until the biggest plants are ready for use, then pull them up, cut the roots off and use them in the salad bowl, they are quite nice.

Radishes are easy enough to grow, provided you sow them in good soil and keep it moist. During the hot weather they like a little shade, otherwise they are inclined to get woody and strong flavoured. The easiest way to grow radishes is to sow the seeds broadcast on a prepared bed, just like sowing annuals, and rake them well into the soil. They are very quick and you can usually begin to pull the biggest of them in about three weeks after sowing. Use as soon as they are big enough or they soon get pithy and mustardy, and then they are not worth eating. There are several varieties to choose from. French breakfast is perhaps as good as any, and you can keep sowing them a few at a time from now till August. Then if you want to continue radishes in the winter, you can sow a bed of the black Spanish variety about August Bank Holiday, thin them out a bit when they come up, and then lift the roots in the autumn and store them in sand like carrots for winter use. They have black skins and not very attractive, but they are quite sweet and crisp. I suppose we mustn't forget mustard and cress, that should always be available, and it's never quite so nice as when you grow it at home. In warm frames or greenhouses you can sow it in boxes about every ten days. You can even grow on the kitchen window sill. You can also sow it out of doors from now till August, but even there you get better results if you make a little frame by knocking the bottom out of a flat box and using the framework with a pane of glass over it. Whether in boxes indoors, or out of doors, you merely produce a surface of fine soil, spread the seeds over it rather thickly and then press them down with a block of wood or something. Don't cover them with soil, otherwise they will lift bits up as they grow, and make your salad gritty, and I can't think of anything more horrible than that. For the rest, all they want is water when necessary, they mustn't get dry, and in hot sunny weather, especially out of doors, it's advisable to put a mat or something over them to shade them till they have germinated. Mustard grows quicker than cress so you shouldn't mix them. It's better to keep them separate and sow the cress two full days before the mustard, then they should be ready for cutting together.

Cucumbers are always welcome in the summer, and you can grow quite good ones out of doors. We call them ridge cucumbers, and although they are not so long and straight and handsome as the greenhouse kinds, the flavour is just as good, and they should not be discarded if they turn a bit yellow or look over-ripe, that is just the nature of them, and when you cut them up you will find them firm and crisp. You can usually buy plants of ridge cucumbers from local nurseries in May, and they should be planted out and given just the same treatment as marrows, the richer the soil the better; of course they don't take up so much room as marrows and you can allow a good square yard to each plant.

You can always keep up a supply of spring onions by sowing a short row or two now, and again in a month's time, and a third time in August; White Lisbon is a good variety for pulling in the young stage. All you do is to sow the seeds thinly in drills and pull the young onions out as they reach the required size. These small onions are not everybody's fancy, I suppose, and we all know their drawbacks, but I believe they are extremely valuable from a food point of view. I was told recently of a famous Scottish peer who was something of an authority on diet, and his gardener bought onion seed by the pound, and sowed it in boxes all the year round. The little thin onions were pulled when they were about three inches long, and washed and trimmed. Then a bunch of these little threadlike onions was placed regularly on the dinner table in a glass by the side of his Lordship's plate. And before starting his meal, he would shake the moisture from the bunch and chew them up with as much relish as if they were a Manhattan Cocktail, probably more. I don't know whether he did it during his honeymoon, or whether he acquired the habit later in life, but he firmly believed that his regular dose of little onions kept him fit, and perhaps they did.

I daresay you have often heard me talk about chives but not many of you grow them. If you found onions a little too strong for your palate, try chives instead.

The leaves chopped up in a salad give it a mild oniony flavour without the pungency or the tears. Many of us, who fight shy of onions, rather like a suggestion of their flavour, in a sort of second-hand way. I shared a dish of soused herrings recently, and we all agreed that they were unusually nice and tasty and began to make inquiries, and discovered that they had been soused in the vinegar from a pot of pickled onions. Well, if you want to get a little of the onion flavour in your salad, grow chives. They are quite easy; you divide up the old clumps and plant them in a row as an edging to your border; they are quite pretty, and have little lilac-coloured flowers; then you pull the outer leaves off as required, and others continue to grow. If you like a mustardy twang in your salad bowl grow a few nasturtium plants and use a few of the half-grown leaves.

I am often asked how to grow watercress in small gardens. Well, candidly, I don't think it is worth the bother, unless you have a stream of clear running water, which very few people have. It's quite true that you can grow it in any dirty old ditch or pool, but whether it is fit to eat is quite another question. Tainted watercress has been known to cause serious illness, but the watercress grown commercially, which you buy in the shops, is grown under such carefully controlled conditions that it is a wholesome and highly valuable article of diet. So for my part I would rather buy it than grow it.

I haven't forgotten the tomato as an essential ingredient of the salad bowl, but it won't be safe to plant out tomatoes in the open till the end of next month, and I shall have something to say about them before then. In the meantime reserve a place for a few plants, in the sunniest and most sheltered position you can find, in front of a wall, facing south, is the ideal spot. Dig out a trench there, about eighteen inches wide and the same in depth, and leave it open so that the spring rain and sunshine can get into it and sweeten and warm the soil. And get your plants ordered, so that when planting time comes you will have some nice big plants in pots, instead of having to start at the beginning with little ones. Time is valuable where outdoor tomatoes are concerned, they have to do a lot in a short time, so the more advanced they are before planting out the sooner shall we get the fruit.

May

THE INVADING ARMY

IT seems a pity to introduce the spirit of war into our peaceful gardens, but I'm afraid there is no help for it, the invaders are forming up their battalions, and we shall have to be on the defensive. This year, above all years, we must do everything possible to keep our crops and plants free from pests and diseases, and the best way to do that is to tackle them early, before they have a chance to dig themselves in. We lose a tremendous amount of stuff every year through pests and diseases, and most of it could be prevented. The trouble is that we don't, as a rule, think about pests until the garden is running alive with them, and then it's too late to do much about it. So let us remember the old saying, "Prevention is better than cure," this year, and resolve to keep the garden clean from the start. I consider that one of the worst of the insect pests is the commonest, the aphis, which in one form or another, either as green fly, black fly, white fly or grey fly, attacks nearly all the plants we grow, and it is not only the direct damage done by the fly itself that we are up against, but the fact that it paves the way for some of the most serious diseases and carries them from one plant to another. If we could keep the garden free from aphis, we should dodge quite a lot of trouble, and aphis is not difficult to destroy. A good syringing with Derris wash or nicotine wash usually settles all the flies it reaches; the trouble is that they breed so fast. We start any time now with the first pairs which hatch out from the eggs which have been stuck on the trees or bushes all the winter.

That's an interesting point about green fly, in the autumn when food is getting scarce the last broods of the season's green flies get busy laying eggs, which remain dormant all the winter and hatch out in the spring; but then, when there are plenty of bursting buds and young leaves about, the green flies don't waste time laying eggs, they produce young direct, and pretty rapidly too; the young ones have large families of their own before they are many days old, and so it goes on. It has been calculated that the first pair which hatch out in the spring can give rise to a family of about a million during a single season. So you see how important it is to catch the first pairs and stop the rush. In the case of many of the diseases we advise spraying before they appear with the object of keeping them away. I'm afraid it isn't much use spraying for green fly before it appears, but it certainly pays to keep your eyes open and as soon as you see the first flies on the roses or on anything else, let them have it, good and strong. It may be any time now, and that early spraying is the most valuable of the lot, especially on the roses; it not only settles the flies, but also catches the first caterpillars which hatch out before they do their dirty work. For the green caterpillars of the winter moth on the fruit trees Derris is the best apray for amateurs, because it is practically non-poisonous, and therefore safe, but remember that it is much easier to destroy caterpillars while they are very young than when they get old and tough.

One of the worst pests of the fruit trees is the saw fly, the pest which puts the maggots in the apples, or at least it's one of them; the codlin moth also does it, but in most districts the saw fly is the greatest culprit. It flies around just after the blossom drops and lays eggs on the tiny undeveloped apples; the eggs soon hatch and the maggots burrow into the little apples and spoil them. One of the best things I know to prevent it is Derris dust, blown through the trees just after the blossom has fallen. You can buy a powder blower for a few shillings, and it doesn't take long to give the trees a dusting; this not only keeps the flies themselves away, but also destroys the newly hatched maggots. Repeat it about a fortnight later, and it should at least reduce the number of maggoty apples very considerably. Look out too for the first spots of woolly aphis on the branches, they look like bits of cotton wool, but under each bit of wool is a colony of beastly little red insects, which suck the life-blood out of the trees, and also let canker and other diseases in. If you brush the spots out with a stiff brush dipped in methylated spirit, you can keep this pest in check, but of course if you wait till the tree is smothered with it, you are up against a pretty tough proposition. Every year I get a few hundred letters from listeners who have heard that you can keep woolly aphis away by planting nasturtiums at the base of the tree so that they climb up the trunk and branches. All I can say is that I have tried it and seen others try it, but I have never known it to make the slightest difference. Perhaps I've been unlucky, but I rather think it is just another of the old garden fallacies which need a lot of faith and imagination before you can get anything out of them.

Another nasty fruit pest is the big bud of black currants. I daresay you have all seen the round swollen buds on the bushes, which fail to open, and turn brown during the summer. These are caused by masses of tiny little mites, too small to be seen with the naked eye, which get in the buds and cripple them, and soon spread over the bushes. In the first place you should pick off all the swollen buds you can find and burn them, not drop them on the ground; then, if the growth is not too far advanced, you can destroy large numbers of the mites by spraying the bushes with strong lime-sulphur, one part to fifteen parts of water. In southern districts I'm afraid it's too late for this, you want to do it when the first leaves are about the size of a shilling, and it will make a nasty mess of them; they will look as if the bushes had been burnt. But they soon recover and the crop is none the worse for it, better indeed, if you can get rid of the wretched mites. But you had better not do it if the leaves are already well advanced. I'm afraid it's my fault if you are too late. I ought to have told you before. Black currants are worth taking care of. Doctors say they are about the most valuable of all the fruits, full of lovely vitamins and things, and cure all sorts of ailments.

I don't know whether I ought to talk about such luxuries as strawberries in war-time, but if you've got a good bed, you may as well look after it and get the best you can from it. Strawberries often get crippled up with a wretched little mite, which is too small to see, but comes in such numbers that it often spoils the plants and ruins the crop if something isn't done about it. A grower said to me the other day that he hoped the January frost had settled the strawberry mite. What a hope! The frost may have busted the waterpipes and killed all the winter greens and spring cabbages and choice shrubs, but I wouldn't mind betting a three-penny bit that all the insects and pests will come up smiling and as full of fight as ever. So look out for the strawberry mite, and give the plants a good dusting once a fortnight, till the flowers are here, with green sulphur; this keeps the mite down and also the mildew, and this is where your powder blower will come in handy again.

I think a good many of you know by this time that I would never suggest any measures which might involve cruelty to birds; in a general way birds do a lot of good in the garden as well as mischief, and I would rather regard them as friends than as enemies. At the same time there are exceptions, and perhaps the worst offender of all is the wood pigeon. Fortunately wood pigeons are very wild and nervous and don't often visit gardens in urban districts; but they do in country places, and if they once invade the garden there is only one thing for it, you must declare war on them and shoot them, for they can very soon ruin a vegetable garden once they start on it. They have played havoc with the green stuff in many gardens recently; what the frost didn't destroy the pigeons did. You don't often see them, because they come at break of day while you are still tucked up in bed; but if you do happen to see wild pigeons in the garden, and you possess a gun, give them a painless end and make a pie of them, or they will collect all the pigeons for miles around and strip your garden of everything worth having. I daresay I shall get a few letters of abuse from so-called nature lovers for saying this, but I can't help it. We are out to grow all the food we can this year, and we must protect it against pests of every kind. If you were a farmer in some parts of the country, you would know only too well what wood pigeons can do. I think there is a lot of luck in the pest world, some pests are very attractive, and therefore get a lot of sympathy and protection, while others, such as the rat, get no sympathy from anybody. Last year a lady told me she was horrified and disgusted when she heard me advocate the shooting of the pretty grey squirrel, then went on to ask if I could recommend a poison to put down for earwigs, which would be harmless to the birds and the cat. Well, why poison the poor innocent earwigs? They can't help being earwigs, and I suppose they have as much right to live as grey squirrels and wood pigeons. We may as well be consistent about it; but I frequently find that the most tender hearted of nature lovers will willingly pour a kettle of boiling water on to an ant's nest, a most horrible form of cruelty, but will carry on like old boots at a naughty, cruel schoolboy who kills a pretty white butterfly. I don't like killing anything, but the fact remains that if we are to grow food crops in our gardens we must destroy their natural enemies, whether pretty or otherwise. Many of the small birds are very troublesome just now, they not only take the seeds, but also pull up the seedlings, and peck the polyanthus flowers all to bits, and so on, but there are ways and means of keeping them away without hurting them. I'm afraid some of the methods employed are not very effective. Festoons of rags and papers merely show the birds where the seeds are, and the news soon spreads. Scarecrows are not much use either. I saw a bird building a nest in one once, which seemed like adding insult to injury. One man tells me he hangs dead jays and magpies about the garden; they may frighten the birds a bit, but I'm afraid I shouldn't fancy corpses like that about the place, especially when they got rather more than dead. Someone sent me a newspaper cutting showing how a gentleman used real cats, stuffed, and stood them about among the vegetables. I don't know how he got the cats, but I know *where* he could get a few—in my back garden, the place fairly stinks of cats, and I'm more concerned with keeping the cats away than the birds, so I'm starting blowing pepper dust about again, it's quite cheap and effective; cat's don't like pepper, but it does them no harm, merely makes them sneeze if they get a good noseful. But to return to the birds. I still think strands of black thread are as good as anything, the birds get a fright when their toes or wings touch the invisible thread, and I have never yet known it to injure one.

There are plenty of pests in the vegetable garden to look out for. Slugs are the most unpopular perhaps, but a few pinches of one of the new metaldehyde slug destroyers among the plants will soon settle them. Then there are the various flies and their maggots, onion fly, carrot fly, parsnip fly, and celery fly. The only way to deal with these is to prevent the flies laying eggs on the crops, and to do this you must make them smell nasty. One simple way is soak a ball of string in paraffin, and stretching it along the rows a few inches above the ground, it doesn't take long, and you needn't put it on every row, just criss-cross it over the crops from one stick to another. Or if you possess a powder blower, a very light dusting of Derris or nicotine dust over the beds about once a week till early June will usually keep them away. The flies find the crops by their keen sense of smell, and if there is something there which smells stronger they pass it by.

You will have noticed that I have already mentioned Derris dust or Derris wash several times. I think it is one of the best of all insecticides for amateurs. It is more or less non-poisonous; you can use it as a dust or as a wet spray, nearly every sundriesman sells it in one form or another, and it seems effective against biting insects such as caterpillars, as well as sucking insects such as green fly. It is quite good as a remedy against that beastly little turnip flea beetle which riddles the leaves with shot holes, and also against the black fly of the broad beans. If you watch out for the first sign of these on the beans, and blow a charge of Derris dust over them, you can easily keep them in check.

Last year the cabbage caterpillars did a tremendous amount of damage. I saw whole crops eaten to ribbons by them. We must try to avoid that this year. A good deal can be done by destroying the white butterflies, to prevent them laying their eggs; the next thing is to destroy the eggs, these are quite easy to see if you turn up the leaves and look for them; they are bright yellow, and are stuck on the undersides of the leaves in groups or clusters, and all you have to do is to squash them, and prevent them hatching into caterpillars. Even if you miss them it's surprising what a lot can be done by picking off the caterpillars whenever you see them. You needn't be afraid of them, they won't bite you. But if you give the plants a good dusting with Derris as soon as you see the first caterpillars I don't think you will be troubled much. This dusting will also check

E

the white fly which has been so bad in the brussels sprouts and other greens of late years. The cabbage root fly sometimes does a considerable amount of damage to the green crops. Perhaps you will notice here and there a wilted plant, turning yellow, and if you pull it up you find a number of white maggots in the root. These are caused by a fly which lays eggs round the base of the plants. The bulletin I mentioned suggests calomel dust sprinkled round the plants immediately after planting. Finely powdered naphthalene is also quite good, a very little sprinkled round each plant will usually keep the fly away. In districts where this root fly is prevalent, sundriesmen often sell small cardboard or felt discs treated with tar; these can be slipped on to the stem of the plant so that they rest flat on the ground and the fly can't lay her eggs there; it sounds a tedious job, but it's surprising how quickly you can do it, and if it's going to save half your plants it's worth doing.

We must keep an eye on the potato crop this year, and try to avoid disasters there. There are so many potato troubles that I could spend a whole afternoon talking about them, but the one which is most likely to be serious is the well-known blight, which ruins the foliage and very considerably reduces the crop. When you sometimes look at a potato crop in the early autumn, with the foliage dead and flat on the ground like so much straw, you are apt to regard it as a normal condition, but it isn't; potato tops ought to be still green at that time, they are brown and dead because they have been killed by blight, and it very often gets down to the tubers and causes them to decay. Even if it only kills

the leaves the crop is very considerably reduced. Taking
the country all round, I believe I am safe in saying that
this disease reduces the potato crop in an average year
by about two tons an acre. Think what that amounts
to all over the country; and it could be prevented if
we would only take the trouble to spray them properly,
and at the right time. I know that potato spraying is
a troublesome and inconvenient business, but after all,
you have already put a good deal of work and time on
the potato crop, and you won't mind that, so why not
take a little extra trouble this year and try to insure them
against disease and loss. The snag about potato spraying
is that it has to be done properly and carefully and at
the right time to be effective; as often as not it is done
in such a slipshod manner that it is a mere waste of
time; then, of course, it is condemned as being useless.
I consider this operation so important in war-time
that I'm going to chance boring you with a few details
about it. Spraying potatoes is a form of insurance; a
preventive measure, not a cure. The leaves of the potato
are covered with a spray to prevent them becoming
infected by the spores of the fungus, which are carried
about in the breeze, and under suitable conditions
germinate on the leaves of potatoes and set up the disease,
which rapidly spreads and destroys the foliage. So in
the first place it is essential that the spraying is done
before the crop is attacked. It doesn't, as a rule, appear
during June, or in dry weather, it is usually after the
first heavy rains in July, when we get a period of thundery,
muggy weather, that blight gets a start, and then it
spreads quickly. So the correct time to spray potatoes
is as soon as the foliage is dry after the first heavy rains

in July, and follow this a fortnight later to cover new foliage which had grown in the meantime. The popular washes are Burgundy mixture and Bordeaux mixture; they are rather similar. Burgundy is one pound copper sulphate, one and three-quarter pounds common soda, and ten gallons water. Bordeaux is one pound copper sulphate, one pound freshly slaked lime, and ten gallons of water. I think Burgundy is the most convenient. The mixing is very important. You must not put the copper and soda together until you are ready to use them; the best way is to dissolve the pound of copper sulphate in eight gallons of water in a wooden tub, and dissolve the one and three-quarter pounds of soda in two gallons of water in a bucket. Then when you are ready to spray empty the bucket into the tub and stir well, and use it immediately. There are also some good proprietary preparations on the market, which merely need diluting with water, but I mustn't mention the names here. The best sprayer, if you can afford one, or borrow one, is a knapsack sprayer, but in a small garden you could manage with a bucket sprayer, or even a syringe. Whichever it is, it should have a fine, misty spray, and you should cover the foliage on the top as well as underneath. Take my tip and have a try at this spraying this year, and if you follow my directions you will get a better crop of potatoes. It would be quite a good idea, while you are using it, to give the outdoor tomatoes a spraying, because they often get the same disease. You might also give the celery an occasional dose, and keep the leaf spot or rust disease away. The worst troubles of peas are the maggots and the mildew. The maggots, which we sometimes find

128

when we shell the peas, and are extremely annoying, are really caterpillars of the Pea Moth. I don't know any real cure for it, although an occasional dusting with Derris helps to keep the moth away. You seem to get it worst on the late peas, and the early ones often dodge it. Many a good row of peas, especially late in the season, is ruined by white mildew. This can, to a large extent, be kept away by dusting the plants occasionally with sulphur, say once a week, before there is any mildew, not after the plants are white with it. I prefer the green sulphur, it is finer and more penetrating and, I think, more effective, and it doesn't make a mess. I use it for mildew on roses as well as vegetables. Flea beetles on turnips and brassica seedlings are sometimes very destructive, especially in dry weather when the plants stop growing. A pinch of sulphate of ammonia, and a good watering will often keep them moving faster than the flea can injure them, and an occasional dusting with Derris will settle the hash of large numbers of them. I am often asked about ants in the garden, or in the house; I've tried a good many things, but the best plan of all is to trace them to their headquarters, usually under the rockery or crazy stones, where you will find great colonies of them rushing round with eggs about three times as big as themselves. I usually get Henry to hold up the stones, while I give them a good plastering with a strong nicotine wash. Last summer we spent half a day at it, and wiped out the whole lot, I didn't notice another ant all through the season.

SUMMER

May

BEES, WEEDS, AND OTHER IMPORTANT MATTERS FOR MAY

I WANT to start to-day with a few words about the busy bees. I don't think we, as gardeners, attach sufficient importance to bees, like many other things they seem to have been very much commercialised in late years, and most people think of them in terms of the honey they produce, which, valuable though it is, ought really to be the secondary consideration. A hive of bees is well worth keeping for the good work they do in the garden. In these days of strife and anxiety, I often let my mind wander back to the old country village, where the orchards and gardens were humming and buzzing with bees, and our old lime tree in June sounded like the deep diapason note of a great organ. People were not so concerned then with scientific methods of bee-keeping, they kept them as part of the garden equipment, taking a little honey when there was any to spare, but at the same time realising that happy, active bees meant good fruit crops. For where there are no bees the blossoms do not get properly pollinated and the fruit crop is short.

I'm not going to attempt to tell you anything about modern methods of bee-keeping, but I do suggest that wherever there is a garden, there ought to be a beehive somewhere in the offing, and like most natural hobbies, you can find a great deal of pleasure and interest in keeping bees. Unfortunately many people are afraid of bees because of that sharp little sting they possess, but as a rule bees are not aggressive; they will defend themselves, but rarely attack, they much prefer to remain neutral and get on with their job. I believe I am right in saying that it kills or seriously injures a bee to sting anyone, and he can only do it once, so he doesn't do it unless he feels obliged to. And when he does, I think the sting of a bee is very much overrated; when I was in the seed trade, we used to put hives of bees in the glasshouses to pollinate cinerarias, and I have often worked with them crawling all over my bare arms. Occasionally I got a sting, but I just rubbed it and took very little notice of it. I don't think it was any worse than a nettle.

I remember years ago watching some men trying to capture a swarm which had settled on a yew tree, and one of them stood underneath, and the whole mass dropped on to him. They covered his head and shoulders and swarmed into his hair and whiskers in their thousands. He must have been either very frightened or very brave and resourceful, for he stood perfectly still while another man drew them all off into a skep, and not one of them stung him. His only remark was that they were very warm. If he had got panicky, and excited, it might have been very different. Well, I don't suppose you will ever find yourselves in quite such an unusual situation, but don't let the fear of a sting prevent you keeping bees, they are well worth while.

Now for a few jobs in the garden. May is an interesting and pleasant month, but it is also a busy one, and among other evil things which come to enjoy its sunny days are the weeds. Weeds of every description, great and small, tough and tender; it's marvellous where they all come from. Up to this year I've been fairly free of creeping convolvulus, or bellbine, but now it has got into the gooseberry patch. If you want to punish anyone for being naughty, just give him an hour or two pulling bellbine out of gooseberry bushes, it should prove very effective. This is the time of the year to tackle weeds with a will, or rather with a hoe. Keep the Dutch hoe busy among the crops and never allow a weed to flower in the garden if you can help it. If you do, it means seeds and another crop of weeds. But unless the weather is very dry, the Dutch hoe is not very effective unless you follow it with the rake and take the weeds away. Just pushing them about with a hoe from one place to another and leaving them there, merely transplants them and they thrive on it. I suppose in a well-kept garden weeds should never be seen at all, they should never get beyond their early infancy. I believe there are a few gardens like that about, but not many. But even if there are no weeds, regular light hoeing between the rows of vegetables is always worth while, especially in dry weather; it prevents a crust forming on the soil surface, and prevents evaporation of moisture.

For weeds on the paths, or between bricks and cobble-stones there are plenty of good weed killers. One of the simplest is Commercial Sodium Chlorate, which I have often mentioned before. Dissolved in water at the rate of one pound to three gallons of water, it will kill practically any weed it touches, and garden plants as well, so be careful where you splash it. It is non-poisonous to animals, but is rather combustible, so handle it carefully and avoid friction, or it may go off with a fizz.

Most of the crops would benefit now by a little tonic in the shape of a sprinkling of fertiliser between the rows. If plants are growing rapidly and strongly, they don't need it, but if they seem to be hanging fire, a light sprinkle of sulphate of ammonia, or one of the appropriate fertilisers, will probably keep them on the move. It is at times when plants slow up and come to a standstill, owing to lack of moisture or nourishment, that the insect pests get the upper hand. That little flea beetle of the turnips and young winter greens, for instance, rarely does much damage to crops which are kept growing, because the leaves grow faster than the fleas can eat them, and although they make holes in them just the same, the growing plants are not seriously affected. But of course if the plants are making no growth, they can't keep pace with the ravages of the fleas. The idea then is to keep them moving with a little fertiliser and water if necessary.

A very important job at this time of the year is the preparation of tender plants for planting out later this month. Flowering plants such as geraniums and dahlias, or marrows, cucumbers and tomatoes, are often kept in the greenhouse or frame too long, and then suddenly transferred to the open ground; then of course they catch a cold, and it takes them a long time to get over the change. From now on they need all the fresh air you can give them, except on frosty nights. Gradually get them hardened off and accustomed to the weather, by taking the lights off the frame, or standing the plants outside whenever conditions are favourable,

E *

then when you plant them out, they won't feel the change.

Talking about marrows, if you haven't already sown them I would suggest the bush varieties for this year in preference to the trailing kinds, especially where space is valuable, because they take up very little room. If you are growing the trailing kinds, it is quite a good plan to follow the old method of growing them on the manure heap, or rather the rubbish or compost heap, or heap of stacked soil; there is hardly likely to be a manure heap in gardens just now. But any heap does, not because a mound is necessary, marrows grow just as well on the flat, but they may as well cover the heap and keep it tidy as occupy valuable garden space. The family air-raid shelter might make a good marrow bed this year. You would have to put a barrow load or two of good rich soil on the top to plant them in and keep it moist, or you could put it at the sides, and train the marrows over the shelter.

To return to bedding plants for a moment, especially such rapid growing things as dahlias, don't let them get starved before you plant them out. I saw some crowded together in a box the other day, and turning yellow. Not only are they half starved and suffering, but it won't be possible to get them out without tearing the roots apart and injuring them. The same applies to tomatoes and any other plants growing in boxes. The temptation is to plant them out too soon, or to leave them huddled up together in the boxes too long. It would pay hand over fist to pot them up if you can manage it, if it's only for two or three weeks, then you needn't hurry with the planting and they won't be suffering. All these things are growing fast now, and if they come to a standstill and get a check, it takes them a long time to get over it.

It is time now for the first row of runner beans to go in, in the south at any rate; seeds, I mean, not plants. If you want some good beans, treat them well. Anybody can get a row of runners without much trouble, but very few crops pay better for a little special attention. Give them the best and deepest soil you can, and sow the beans nine inches apart in a double row; put them in a good inch deep, and don't water them before they are up, they don't like it. When you sow them, put in a few extra somewhere else, so that if anything happens to one here and there you can plant another in its place, otherwise, at nine inches apart, you might get some conspicuous gaps. You can also sow another row of peas, and while the peas are growing, right up till the peas are forming, give them an occasional syringing with soot water. I don't know whether it's a fad of mine, but I always imagine that soot keeps peas clean and healthy, gives the foliage and the pods a better colour, and helps to keep the maggots away. You can give the beans a dose too, and also water them with it, it does them good. The best way to make it is to put a bag of soot into a tub of water, poke it about well with a stick and leave it for a day or two, and then dilute each can of water with it. It makes it quite black, but that doesn't matter, you are not likely to use it too strongly.

Look out for the first signs of black fly on the broad beans. It may not be about yet, but it won't be long, as soon as the beans are in full flower, nip out the tuft of growth at the top of each plant, it not only robs the flies of their favourite breeding place, but it throws the strength of the plant into the beans instead of new growth. It also makes quite a nice vegetable dish, if you cook it like spinach. I wonder how many of you have cooked broad beans whole, pod and all, or sliced up like runner beans? If you haven't, try a boiling this year as soon as they are beginning to be big enough and see what you think of them. You have to take them young, of course, before the beans have formed in them. You can take it from me they are very tasty, and in a normal year one of the earliest vegetables you can get. I am often being asked about the soya bean, and many readers suggest that we ought to grow it because of its high food value. That would be all right if we could rely on getting a crop of it, and we can, sometimes, in a very favourable season, but I'm afraid it is too uncertain for war-time purposes. Perhaps in a few years' time, when it has had a bit more breeding and development, it may become a very popular garden crop, but not yet. Every year I receive specimens of blue or purple podded peas and beans, asking me if they are freaks. There is nothing uncommon about them, the bean is one of the climbing French beans, and it turns green when cooked. The purple podded pea has green peas inside it, not of very superior quality. Its only good point, so far as I know, is that the birds don't seem to go for it, which in some districts is an advantage. You can get seeds from most of the big seed firms. Henry grew some peas last year with pods eight inches long. He had two varieties, one called V.C. and the other Quite Content. They were both giants, but then Henry is a past master at growing peas, and any other vegetables for that matter. He is a wise old man in his way; he refuses to read a gardening book, or go to a lecture, or listen to the wireless. He says there's more bunkum written and talked about gardening than anything else on earth. Perhaps he's right, he can certainly grow better vegetables than I can; perhaps he works a bit harder.

Late May

TOMATOES

I suppose nearly everyone who has a kitchen garden, or even an allotment, would like to grow a row of tomatoes this year, so let us discuss them for a few minutes. Under glass, tomatoes are fairly easy and profitable to grow; but out of doors they must always be regarded as something of a gamble, except in very well-favoured districts. I have grown some excellent crops in a back garden in the London area. One year I got fifty-five pounds of ripe fruit from twelve plants; but that was a record year for me, and it doesn't often come off. What we have to remember is that the tomato is a sub-tropical plant and requires warm sunny conditions to bring it to perfection. We don't often get a summer which is long enough and warm enough to see a tomato plant right through its life from start to finish out of doors. It has been known, but it is very rare, and I could tell you a rather interesting story in this connection. I remember one very warm summer, a farmer friend of mine had dressed a small field in the spring with sludge from the local sewage works, and this stuff must have been full of tomato seeds, for they came up all over the field. He sowed mangolds, but they came up so badly, and the tomatoes came up so strongly, that he abandoned the mangold idea and decided to let the tomatoes grow, and grow they did, and during that September he marketed a crop which paid him far better than the mangolds would have done. I don't suppose such a thing would happen more than once in a lifetime, but that happened to be an ideal summer, free from frosts between May and October. If we could rely on such summers, tomato growing out of doors might be a very profitable business. As it is, we have to make the most of the short summers we get, and start the plants under glass so that they are already well advanced before we plant them out. That to my mind is the secret of growing tomatoes out of doors. It is never really safe to plant them out till the end of May or early June, and if at that time they are only small seedlings, it takes them best part of the summer to grow up, and by the time they start fruiting the autumn is on us and the fruit doesn't develop and ripen properly.

But if the plants are well advanced, or grown up and approaching the fruiting stage when you plant them out, you will have saved a good deal of valuable time, and before July is out you may be gathering tomatoes. So take my tip and make sure of good plants, even if they cost a bit more, and get them in pots if you possibly can. A plant knocked out of a pot can be planted without disturbing the roots and giving it a check, but young plants crowded together in boxes, with the roots all tangled together can't be transplanted without injuring the roots, and it takes them some time to get over the operation.

Another important point is to make sure that the plants are properly hardened off. To take them straight from a greenhouse and plant them out of doors is asking for trouble. A few cold nights and they get pneumonia or something, and take a long time to get better. They ought to be standing out of doors now, except on cold nights when frost is likely, getting themselves acclimatised and ready for the change. All these are details, I daresay, but they are just the details which make all the difference between success and failure, and we can't afford failures in war-time. Now, a word about the soil; obviously, as we are asking the tomato plant to do a good deal for us in the shortest possible time, it follows that we must do all we can to help it, and as it is a pretty strong feeder, we must provide the necessary food supply, in the shape of good soil and a properly balanced ration in the way of fertilisers. I know that many of you don't like me to talk about manures and such things while you are eating your pudding, but I don't see how we can get away from it; it's such an essential part of the business.

Now the commonest mistake of all is to pack the soil with strong food and fertiliser before planting, and give no more afterwards. It causes the plants to spurt into a mass of soft tender growth which is of no use whatever, and has to be picked off. The ideal to aim at is to start the tomatoes off with a nicely balanced ration, and then add to it as growth increases, so that the harder the plants are working the more food they will be getting.

So I suggest that you start preparing the soil at once In the first place select the warmest and most sheltered spot you can find; then for each plant, dig out a nice wide hole, at least a foot deep, or if you are planting a row, you can dig a trench. Break up the bottom, so that the drainage is good, and if you can get it, put a layer of good old farm muck along the bottom; if you can't get that, a little hop manure is quite a good substitute. This is a sort of reserve supply and the roots won't get down to it till the plants are in need of it. Then when you fill up the holes or the trench, mix a little good fertiliser with the soil. Those made from fish or poultry manure are quite good; sprinkle them over the soil a little at a time as you fill it in, so that each plant gets about a quarter of a pound well mixed with the soil all round it. At the same time add a little sulphate of potash, one ounce round each plant and even distributed, and also one ounce of superphosphate. Potash is most important for tomatoes, they use far more of it than most crops; if you don't give them enough, you get tomatoes with green and yellow patches on them, and all sorts of other troubles, and you get long jointed soft growing plants with very little fruit, so don't forget the potash, but don't overdo it, or you may make the plants hard and seriously check the growth. It is possible to buy ready prepared tomato fertilisers, with the potash and other ingredients in their proper proportions, and for beginners, or busy people who don't want to be bothered with mixing odds and ends, I think these are the most satisfactory. You usually find directions for use on the tins or packets, and if you follow them, you won't go far wrong. Don't overdo the first supply before planting; the better method is to feed them as they grow, either with weekly doses of liquid manure, or by sprinkling a little tomato fertiliser round the plants and watering it in.

Now I suppose you'll want to know what I mean by liquid manure. Well, the best way to make that is to get a tub of water and drop into it a bag of poultry or other good manure. Poke it about a bit and wait a day or two

YOUR GARDEN IN WAR-TIME

for it to dissolve, and then add a little to each can of
water when you water the plants, just enough to make
the water muddy or cloudy. Frequent weak doses are
better than strong doses at long intervals. It's a dirty,
smelly business, I must admit, and perhaps most of you
would prefer the fertiliser method, which is just as effective, as long as you don't get too heavy handed with
it. There is no need to start feeding till the first little
tomatoes have formed, about the size of peas, and when
you gather the first ripe fruits it's time to stop feeding.

The best time to plant is at the very end of this
month, if the weather is favourable; if it happens to be
snowing then or very wet and cold wait a week or two.
Before you plant give the roots a good soaking, and
plant firmly, and slightly on the deep side; and if you
put each plant in a saucer-shaped depression, you will
not only find it easier to water them later on, but you
can pull the soil up round the stems if necessary and
induce them to send out new roots.

Before you plant, put a good strong stake in position,
about three feet high, and plant your tomato in front
of it. This is better than driving it in after planting,
and perhaps damaging the roots. Keep the plant tied
to the stake as it grows, but don't tie it too tightly, or
the stem won't be able to swell from time to time.
Give a good soaking after planting to settle the soil
round the roots.

The next job will be training, and this is very important
with outdoor tomatoes, but at the same time very simple.
There isn't time to allow the plant to grow in its own
sweet way; if you did nothing to it you would soon
have long fat shoots flopping about all over the place,

142

and by the time they began to bear fruit we should be in the autumn and it wouldn't ripen. So we aim at concentrating all the energy of the plant into producing a moderate amount of fruit instead of an abundance of new growth. We do this by picking out all the young side shoots as they appear, keeping only the main stem with its bunches of flowers and fruit. Mind you, don't pick them off by mistake; still I don't suppose you would do that, as they are easily distinguished. Sometimes the first truss of bloom is very low down and the tomatoes get splashed with mud. If it isn't a very good truss you might cut it off before it develops. You must use your own discretion about that. I cut them off if they are very low down, because I think they rob the later trusses and delay them, and the one or two odd fruits you get early are hardly worth the sacrifice. However, if it is a good truss with several tomatoes on it, by all means leave it. When the plant has produced four nice trusses of bloom it is advisable to pick the top out and not allow any more new growth at all. After that, all you will have will be the main stem, leaves and bunches of fruit. If you were sure of a warm sunny autumn, you could let it grow a bit taller and produce more trusses of bloom. In a greenhouse, you would do that, but out of doors the chances are that those later trusses would be too late to ripen the fruit, and it is better to be satisfied with four branches of good fruit which gets ripe. If you get four bunches to a plant you won't do so badly. Always gather the fruit as soon as it turns colour; if you leave it to get dead ripe on the plant it robs those which are following on. Some people strip all the leaves off the plants after the fruit has set. I don't know why. It seems a stupid idea to me; it's all very well to cut off a leaf or half a leaf here and there to let the sun get at the fruit, but fruit can't develop properly without leaves, and there is nothing gained by cutting them all off.

June

THINNING, AND OTHER JUNE INTERESTS

THE time has arrived now when we ought to begin to see the results of the spring sowing and planting, and one of the results, as far as I have been able to see, is that many of the crops have come up much too thickly. I am sure that one of the urgent jobs to be tackled is that of thinning out. Beginners, as a rule, don't like thinning ; they often start off by being too heavy handed with the seeds, so that the rows of vegetables come up as thick as mustard and cress, and even when they thin them out, they often leave far more than can do themselves justice. I admit that it takes a bit of courage to tackle a nice healthy looking row of seedlings and pull about three-quarters of them out; it looks a terrible slaughter when you've finished, but it is really necessary if you want good crops. Take any vegetable you like, turnips, parsnips, onions, or lettuces, most people, even the novices, know more or less how big these things are when they are fully grown, so you must give them room to fill out and spread without squeezing each other. If you don't, they can't make good specimens, I daresay by this time you have all got a book or pamphlet of some kind, which tells you how far apart the various vegetables should be, so there is no need for me to go into details about it, but take my tip and thin out drastically if necessary, you won't lose anything by it. Another important point is to do the thinning early, as soon as you can handle the seedlings comfortably; if you leave them too long, the roots get tangled together, and you can't pull one out without injuring the next. Do the thinning when the soil is wet, they come out much easier then; if it is dry, give it a soaking before you start, and water again, if you can, after you've finished, it settles the soil round the roots of those you have left.

I have walked round a good many allotments and vegetable gardens lately, and in most cases I have seen rows of peas coming up much too crowded, in many rows the plants are less than an inch apart. You can't expect a full crop of peas like that; they will look quite good for a time, and they will probably bear a nice lot of pods to begin with, but they will be all over in about a week, because they won't have enough strength to continue cropping. Let me make a suggestion; if your rows of peas have come up very thickly, pull a lot of them out, so as to leave the others three or four inches apart at least; you won't like doing it, but you'll get a better crop of peas, and they will last longer. When you pull the young peas out, if they are only a few inches high, you may be able to plant them somewhere else if you handle them carefully, but it's a bit of a gamble, and perhaps hardly worth the bother, except to fill up gaps in the existing rows. But in any case don't throw them away, cut the lower parts off and then wash the young tops and cook them like spinach; they make quite a tasty dish. I sometimes go over a row of peas when they are growing well and pick out some of the young side shoots to prevent overcrowding, but I don't throw them away, I eat them, and they are very nice too, if you get them while they are young and tender.

I wonder how many of you have tried the so-called

sugar pea. This is grown in the same way as ordinary peas, but instead of waiting for the peas, you pick them fairly young and eat pods and all. They have improved a good deal in recent years, and there is none of the stringiness which you get in the pods of ordinary varieties; most of the best seed firms sell them, and there is still time to sow a row, they don't take up much room.

A little careful thinning in the fruit garden is also well worth while, if you've got a heavy set. Apples, pears, and especially peaches, give a better sample and a heavier crop if the fruits are spaced out comfortably. Professional gardeners nearly always thin out the fruits to about six inches apart. In many gardens the wretched saw fly is thinning out the apples for us; it is still active laying its eggs on the young apples, and it won't be long before they are maggots inside them, so get that dry sprayer and puff some more Derris dust through the trees, that will prevent quite a lot of the trouble.

If you've got a nice row of raspberries coming along, especially if they are out in the full sunshine and inclined to get dry, give them a mulch of something if you possibly can. Of course farmyard manure is the ideal stuff for the job, but one hardly dares to mention such precious stuff now; any old rotten stuff does, old leaf mould or even lawn mowings; it isn't so much a question of feeding as of conserving moisture and keeping the roots cool and comfortable during the hot weather. The roots of raspberries are all quite near the surface; they really belong to the shady woods, and they dry up very quickly in the full sun. If you can cover the roots over with a layer of something the crop will last as long again. If you use fresh lawn mowings, stir it up with a rake now and then, otherwise as it ferments it gets slimy and hot and smelly. Talking of lawn mowings reminds me of that compost heap. During the summer you are pretty sure to get a lot of waste stuff, such as cabbage leaves, carrot tops, weeds, and so on; the dustbin isn't the place for them, nor is the bonfire; the best plan is to start a heap in a corner somewhere, or dig a pit, or even make a sort of bin with four pieces of corrugated iron or old doors or something, and a few good strong posts, and put all the rubbish in that, and each time you put a load in, sprinkle a little calcium cyanide over it, it puts some goodness into it, and helps it to rot down quicker, so that by the time the autumn digging comes round again, you will have a useful heap of stuff to go back into the soil. It's surprising what a lot of things can go into that heap: hedge clippings, for instance, tea leaves, egg shells, anything in fact which is no use for pig or poultry food, even old worn-out socks and the paper you brought the fish and chips home in. It seems to me, that what with the garden compost heap, the cottage pig and poultry and the waste paper collection, there ought to be precious little to put into dustbins now.

A correspondent tells me that he caught eight hundred slugs in his garden in two days. That sounds like good going, but it must be rather a tedious job. For my part, I have been using the new metaldehyde slug destroyer with good results. I bought a tin of it, it looks something like coarse oatmeal, and I just put a pinch of it here and there among the plants; very little does, the slugs soon find it, and disappear. I don't know whether the blackbirds and starlings take them; if they do it does them no harm. I have quite a number of half-tame birds in my garden and they are all fit and well. Henry says the birds are a darned sight more nuisance than the slugs. I think ants have been my biggest trouble this year, but we seem to be getting the better of them. I tried a mixture of borax and icing sugar on them, they seemed to like it, and I daresay it settled a few, but it is difficult to tell. Then we discovered that their headquarters were under the rockery and crag-stones, thousands of them, eggs as well, so while Henry held up the stones, I puffed a good dose of nicotine dust all over them and dropped the stone back into place again, it didn't take us long and it seems to have cleared them. Here is a recipe for a poison bait for ants, which was sent to me by a lady correspondent who has used it with great success on the large wood ants; it seems successful so far with the red ants, would you like to make a note of it? One pound of sugar (that's a snag to begin with, but we need very little, so let us reduce it and make it a quarter). Very well, quarter of a pound of sugar, one ounce of honey, one ounce of arsenate of soda, and half a pint of water. Boil it all together, and then soak small sponges or bits of cotton wool with it, and put it under pots or somewhere where the ants can find it. To quote my correspondent, "The ants take the mixture home to feed the Queen and the royal infants, thus scuppering the whole community in one operation." Sounds interesting, doesn't it; but there's one thing you must remember, arsenate of soda is poison, and must be handled with care.

Another trouble to watch for is celery rust. Poor old Henry had so much of it last year, that I believe he lies awake at nights worrying about it. It's a nasty disease, and a difficult one to deal with once it gets going. The best plan is to try to keep it away by syringing the plants about once a week with Bordeaux mixture, or one of the advertised copper solutions; you needn't drown them, just a light covering over and under the leaves is enough, and this seems to keep slugs away as well as rust. I found last year where we used Bordeaux mixture, the stems were clean and free from blemishes. I may be wrong, but I believe celery rust is encouraged by over-feeding. We know celery can take a good deal of nourishment, especially in liquid form, but you can overdo, and make the leaves so soft and juicy that the disease spreads much more rapidly.

There is one thing I would like to suggest just now, and that is, that it might be well worth while for all amateurs or beginners to carry a little notebook with them and collect useful information for future use. On allotments, for instance, you may have been a bit doubtful this year as to which varieties of peas or lettuces or potatoes to grow, and it is very desirable to get those which suit the locality. So when you are walking round, and you see an extra good crop of something on a neighbour's plot, ask him which variety it is, and make a note of it. As you look round, you often see little things which would be well worth copying, but if you merely commit them to memory and resolve to do it yourself, you will probably forget all about it by next spring. A well-kept notebook can be of very great value. There is always something to learn in gardening, even for old timers. I have picked up some very useful tips from allotment holders, and I find they are always willing to give information. I hope, too, that those who ave had experience will offer helpful suggestions now and then to novices; there are sure to be many mistakes made this year, but perhaps they can be avoided next year, if we do what we can to help each other.

In the flower garden, too, we have done a bit of thinning out and discarded a good many plants. We shall want our flower gardens again one of these days, and when we restock them it may as well be with the best, so it wouldn't be at all a bad idea to take notes now and then of any good tree, shrub, or plant which appeals to us; we may be very glad of that notebook later on.

I was talking about thinning vegetables. There is another kind of thinning in the flower borders which ought to be attended to just now, disbudding. If we want the roses and carnations to be good ones, we should remove some of the smaller buds which cluster round the centre flowers. One bloom to a stem means a fine rose or carnation, so don't be afraid to nip off the side buds, and the younger they are when you do it, the better. The less the number of flowers on a plant, the better they usually are, and especially if you want to cut them, disbudding should not be neglected.

THE ORIGIN OF GARDEN VEGETABLES

WE are thinking a good deal about vegetables in these times, and vegetables are going to play an important part in feeding the nation. But do you ever wonder how they all found their way into out gardens, or into cultivation? Or when you walk into a shop and buy a packet of seeds do you ever wonder how they got there? I rather think we take a great deal for granted in gardening and accept all the good things as a matter of course; so long as we can buy the plants and seeds we require, it's none of our business as to how they are produced, anymore, perhaps, than when we buy a pair of shoes. All the same I think it is rather interesting sometimes to think over these matters, so let us talk of vegetable seeds for a few minutes, and how they find their way so conveniently into the seed shops. First look at the vegetables themselves. I daresay many of you are growing a dozen different kinds, all perfectly developed plants supplying wholesome and palatable food, where have they come from? You don't find many of them growing in the wild state anywhere in the world. If one of these plants could answer for itself it would probably tell you that, generations ago, it lived in a wild state, or its ancestors did, but compared with itself, its ancestor was a small insignificant weed, and it owes its development and its present standard of excellence to the guiding hand of man, to the patience, skill and perseverance of gardeners. Gardeners, as a class, don't cut much ice in the general order of things, they are usually depicted by cartoonists and others as whiskery old men with grubby necks, and in normal times they are accepted or tolerated as a matter of course and very little notice is taken of them. But in war-time they become rather important, and we begin to realise that they have their uses after all. As a matter of fact, gardeners of the past have made it possible for us to cultivate our gardens to-day, and to dig for victory, and to them and their work we owe all the vegetables we are so enthusiastically growing. It is rather interesting to trace, if we can, the development of any particular vegetable from the wild state to the plants as we know them to-day. You have to use your imagination a bit to do it, although in some cases you can still find the original plants growing wild, the wild parsnip or cabbage, for instance, and compare them with their modern types; they will often provide an interesting object lesson. What's more, the history of a plant is a guide to its cultivation. A plant whose wild ancestors grew on limey soil may require a lot of lime if it is to avoid various diseases like club-root, and the opposite is true in the case of a plant which is a native of a sour soil.

But let us try to cast our minds or our imaginations back towards the beginning, to those far-off days of primitive man. I don't know what he lived on, perhaps anything he could get, flesh, fish or fowl, but it is reasonable to suppose that he would also find that certain leaves, plants or roots were good for food, and that some were better than others, and being intelligent he would probably collect seeds or roots of the best of them and plant them nearer his home to save long journeys, and he would have to clear away useless vegetation to make room for them, and give them a little special attention. In response to this, and free from competition of other wild plants, they would grow into better specimens; no doubt the man would learn a good deal about them and their requirements by constant observation, and so began the art of cultivation. It is reasonable to suppose also that man would soon begin to select the best specimens to save seed from, and by continuous selection, the plants would improve in the way he wanted them to; thus, if he ate the root, he would naturally select those with the biggest or best flavoured roots, and so on. Then by growing together different types of the same plant he would soon begin to observe changes in the seedlings, and would learn something about cross pollination and breeding, and its possibilities. So you see, it needs no great stretch of imagination to see how the breeding of vegetables first began, and how it developed, until it became a fine art, or rather an exact science, as it is to-day.

Let us take one or two examples, peas for instance, which are perhaps the oldest of the cultivated vegetables. They are said to have been grown by the Greeks 3000 years before Christ. The wild pea can still be found growing in Palestine, but it is a funny little thing compared with the peas as we know them; it is a slender growing little plant with tiny pods, each containing only three or four little seeds. There are records that these were grown in Tudor times, as a rare and costly dish for Queen Elizabeth and her ladies, but strangely enough it was not till about 1800 that the breeding of peas was undertaken seriously and systematically. Since that time wonderful strides have been made and from that original little plant scores of varieties well known to all of you have been developed, some tall, some dwarf, and some with pods containing anything up to a dozen peas, vastly different in nearly every respect to their early ancestors. Not so very long ago, as time goes, peas were a costly luxury, enjoyed only by the rich; now we can all enjoy them, and much better flavoured ones than they had. We get them fresh from the gardens and allotments all the summer, and from tins all the winter, or dried, or as pea soup or peas pudding. And we have to thank gardeners for that.

Another interesting example of development is the Cabbage or Brassica family, which has produced some very striking variations. If you walk along some of our southern cliffs you may come across the wild form of the cabbage or brassica. It is a rather insignificant plant botanically known as *brassica oleracea,* rather resembling a small kale, and it is said to be the ancestor of all the cabbage and winter greens of our gardens. When this plant was brought into cultivation, away from its hard life on the cliffs, away from competition and the laws of the survival of the fittest, it began to produce remarkable changes in its seedlings. I suppose in wild life, where we often find variations in seedlings, many of them which might show new and interesting characters, are not strong enough to survive the struggle for existence; or if they do they rarely produce a second generation, but under the more comfortable and protected conditions of a cultivated garden they have a better chance. The seedlings from this wild brassica plant began to show variations, which were observed and encouraged; some showed a tendency to cluster their leaves together in the centre, and so the cabbage was developed, others grew taller and produced new shoots all over the stems and became kales, in others the shoots closed up into solid balls and we got brussels sprouts, others produced flower shoots very early and gave rise to broccoli, and so on. All this didn't happen in a season, or in a generation. It took many generations of patient selection, and many disappointments and setbacks were experienced during the gradual development of the distinct types as we know them to-day, but there they are, and now we all grow them easily enough, and they have added enormously to our food supply. These are just two examples; the same story can be told of all our cultivated vegetables. They have all been developed from wild plants, either British or foreign, and the work is still going on. For all I know future generations may be eating an improved form of chickweed or thistle, they would be no more remarkable than our present-day vegetables.

All this may sound as if the job has been well done, and all we have to do now is to sit back and enjoy the results; that may be so as far as most of us are concerned, but the work of those who produce the seeds for us goes on as strenuously as ever. It is not enough to have reached the present standard of excellence in vegetables, they have got to maintain it, which is just as big a job. These things don't remain stationary; and these highly developed vegetables, if left to breed and seed in Nature's own sweet way, very soon begin to drift back towards the wild state again. The bees and other agencies which do the pollinating, don't employ any particular method of selection. A friend of mine once planted all the members of the brassica family together and allowed them to flower and seed. The seed produced some startling results; many of them were unlike anything in cultivation, most of them were inferior. There were brussels sprouts with cabbages on the top, red savoys and all sorts of odd looking things, but none of them much use from a kitchen point of view, and the experiment showed quite clearly that although the different forms of these plants had probably taken hundreds of years to develop and fix, the whole of that work could be undone in one season, by allowing the plants to cross and seed indiscriminately. In the production of seeds, these plants have to be carefully isolated from each other, or the next generation will deteriorate. A crop of beet, for instance, can be spoilt, from a seed point of view, if there is a field of mangel-wurzels within half a mile of it. Many years ago I was associated with a large seed firm, whose seed trial grounds were quite near to a field of allotments, and this firm gave the allotment holders seeds free of charge on one condition, that they never allowed certain of their vegetables to flower. Had they done so, they might easily have been crossed with the firm's pedigree strains and rendered them impure.

Every year crops of the different vegetables are grown by the large seed firms, and during the growing season these are subjected to a process of careful selection. Only the perfect plants, true to type, are marked for keeping as seed parents, all the others being destroyed before they flower.

The Mother seed, so carefully obtained from selected plants, is grown under isolated conditions and, while

F

growing, any untrue plants are taken out; this is what seedsmen call rogueing. The resultant seed crop is duly harvested, and then goes through an elaborate process of cleaning, to remove all impurities, small or light seeds, or anything which ought not to be there, and very wonderful and cunning some of these cleaning machines are. After all this, the Government steps in, and insists that samples of every stock of seeds must be tested to make sure that they germinate well and are true to type. Most of the big seed firms have done this for generations, for their own satisfaction and for your benefit, and they also grow a few rows of every stock of vegetable seeds they sell, so that they can keep records of the results. Finally, the selected, cleaned, and tested seeds are weighed or measured, and put into their pretty packets. It is safe to say that in the case of every reputable British seed firm, everything possible has been done to ensure that those packets of seeds shall give you every satisfaction. This year they have worked under great difficulties in their efforts to deliver the goods as usual, and as long as it is humanly possible, I know they will continue to do so. There are years of experience and a great deal of work and worry behind that packet of seeds. The rest is up to you. Treat them carefully, and don't grumble if they cost a penny more than you think they ought to, it is the final result that matters.

to me that the object of my talks lately has been to deal with this subject; either these gentlemen have not troubled to listen, or I must have been making a poor sort of job of it. There are also several asking me to suggest a design for the new garden; quite a number asking me if I can find them a job, and others asking me to recommend the best firm for various garden requirements. All these I'm afraid I must respectfully decline; it isn't quite my job, and while on this point I would like to advise listeners that nearly every county has its advisory services, and the local horticultural adviser, usually located at the offices of the County Council, will always give free advice on matters relating to the garden and allotment, especially food production, and having a knowledge of local conditions, their advice is more reliable than mine. Now, to get down to a few of the more interesting subjects. A few weeks ago I suggested the formation of village allotment societies, with the object of producing more food, and sending their surplus non-perishable vegetables to help the urban populations who are unable to grow anything themselves. In a general way this idea is extremely popular, but I suppose there are always two sides to a question, and a few market gardeners have written calling me dreadful things, and accusing me of taking the bread out of their mouths and so on. Well, I refuse to believe that these few represent the opinions of market gardeners generally. I refuse to believe that the average market gardener wants to see the general public go short of winter vegetables so that he can reap a harvest of higher prices; there may be a few like that, but not many. Most of them I know are only too anxious to co-operate in these

160

dangerous times in doing everything possible to produce more and more food to meet the urgent and growing demand. All my correspondents call my attention to the low prices they have received for brussels sprouts and cauliflowers this year, but we are not concerned so much with perishable crops of that kind when we ask allotment holders to grow more. We are thinking of winter supplies : onions, carrots, peas and beans for drying, and potatoes, which up to last year have been imported from foreign countries to the tune of many million pounds every year. How is this deficiency to be made up? Can the market gardeners do it? I very much doubt it. Neither can the allotment holders even if they crop their land to full capacity. My opinion is that every bushel of winter food that can be produced will be needed. We may have to eat more vegetables instead of less, to make up for some of the other foods which we can no longer get. It is only by all pulling together and making every bit of vacant land produce its full quota that we can get enough, and the more that is produced in or near the place where it is consumed, the greater the saving of transport, and the better it will be for everybody. Apart from possible gluts of seasonable perishable stuff, I'm pretty sure there will be room next winter for all that the market gardeners can grow. I have been connected with market gardening most of my life. I know something of the difficulties, and I should be very sorry to do or say anything which might injure those who are engaged in it; but I happen to know that many of the best-known market growers are whole-heartedly supporting the Dig for Victory campaign, because they realise that this is war, war to the death, and the needs of the nation must come first. Food, or the lack of it, is going to be one of the deciding factors in this business, and it may well be that the market growers and allotment holders will be able to drive the last nail into the Nazi coffin. So much for that. Now, strangely enough, I have had quite a number of letters from private gardeners complaining about their employers. One here says that his employer is always interfering, cutting down supplies, or ordering things for the garden without first consulting him. Really, I don't see what I can do about it. After all, employers have their tastes and opinions, and perhaps they sometimes feel that they are entitled to a say in the matter. Employers are not finding things too easy just now, and I'm rather afraid that the good old days of the autocratic gardener are coming to an end. There was a time when the Duchess dare not cut a rose without first asking the gardener. I knew one who always kept the key of the vineries and peach houses and wouldn't allow his employers in unless he was there to watch over their movements. We used to have an old gardener in our village who took such a pride in his gravel paths that he was quite annoyed if anybody walked on them, and her ladyship frequently walked on the grass to avoid disturbing the peace. Another gardener I knew gave his lady notice because she insisted on having scarlet geraniums in the flower beds, he called it intolerable interference. But I'm afraid that this was in the good old days when gardens were gardens and gardeners were gardeners. They are getting fewer and fewer now I'm afraid, and the prospects of a career in private gardening are getting less and less. But it's no use moaning about it, money is less plentiful than it used to be, and we must adapt ourselves to the changing times.

All this reminds me that ladies frequently write to me about their daughters who want to take up horticulture as a career. There are a great many girls in the gardening profession now, and some of them don't do so bad; for a healthy, interested girl there is a lot to be said for a gardening career. There are possibilities of making a good living, especially in the florist or nursery business, but we must always remember that garden work is no picnic when you have to make a living at it. If a girl specialised in one good line—say violet growing or carnations, or even herbs and salads, she might do very well in normal times. Designing and building rock gardens and other gardening features offers possibilities. In any case I should advise a girl to work for herself if possible rather than seek employment as a private gardener. I am afraid there is very little prospect there. I don't want to turn a girl away from a gardening career, far from it, it has many compensations even if you don't make money, and I think this war is proving that there are not many jobs a man can do that a girl can't do equally well; but my advice to a girl is, unless your heart is really in it, try something else, or you may be in for a disillusionment. There are, of course, some good colleges where girls are trained in horticulture, one at Swanley in Kent and one at Studley in Warwickshire, and no doubt a term or two at one of these would soon help a girl to make up her mind.

This year, as usual, I have received a large number of inquiries about the fruits which appear on the so-called japonica tree. This was a good summer for them, and for some weeks nearly every post brought me a few asking me if they were of any use. I had enough to have made several pots of jelly. These hard, green fruits are really a kind of quince—*Cydonia japonica,* and they make a very nice jelly. It is of a clear orange-red colour, although there is no such colour in the fruits, and the flavour is very distinctive and pleasant. We have made a lot of jam and jelly from ordinary yellow quinces this year, and I have been surprised to find so many people who have never tasted it. To my mind it is one of the nicest of all the preserves. We used one occasionally in an apple pudding while they were about, and it made quite a difference to the flavour. *Cydonia japonica,* apart from its fruits, which are never very plentiful, is one of the nicest plants for climbing on a low wall, nicest because it flowers so early in March, when its red, pink and orange flowers are very welcome. There is one variety called *Cydonia Maulei,* which makes a rather low-growing bush and bears orange-red flowers followed by rather small fruits which ripen a rich yellow colour, and are very sweetly scented. If you collect a bowlful of them and put them in a warm room they last a long time and fill the room with a pleasant perfume.

Now I don't want to get morbid, but I frequently get letters asking me to suggest something suitable for planting on a grave, something low growing, which will stay put without much attention. Usually the kind of grave referred to is a sort of rectangular bed surrounded by a stone or marble curb, and a plant is wanted which will keep tidy and within the prescribed limits. Well, most plants spread about a little if left to themselves, but some decidedly more than others. I should think the mossy saxifrages would be quite nice. They are always neat and green and bear attractive flowers in May. The same applies to the ordinary pink thrift, a little trim up once a year would be all the attention required. The sempervivums (houseleeks), especially some of the fancy varieties, would be ideal. They live on almost nothing, and beyond an occasional one here and there straying over the border line, they would rarely need any attention. A rather nice idea, I think, would be to get a rough stone or two and build a miniature rockery, such as you sometimes see in old stone sinks. You could plant them with thyme, small pinks, silver saxifrages and other little rock plants, and produce a very pretty and permanent effect. For a grave which is just a simple mound of earth, I can think of nothing nicer than a covering of one of the small-leaved trailing ivies, with snowdrops and chionodoxas planted under it to come up every spring. I am not very keen on the ambitious colour schemes often seen on graves, but that of course is just a matter of taste. What I am rather keen on is the beautifying of village churchyards; what a lot of them you see without a flower in them, and yet with a few willing hands and a little ingenuity, you could have borders of lilies, roses and other flowers around the church and in the angles of its walls, lilacs, mock orange, cherries, and other flowering shrubs and trees here and there, and flower borders alongside the paths. Churchyards are usually in prominent places, and I think it would greatly add to the charm of many a village if its ancient church were surrounded by a flower garden instead of sombre

F*

many as we can, although some of us would probably never have bothered about them if they had been plentiful and cheap. I saw a crowd round a confectioner's shop recently because it had become known that they had a stock of chocolate. I wonder if they all really wanted chocolate? Now the word has gone round that onion seed is scarce, and we are asked to use it very carefully. The result is that a great many people are ordering far more than they require, and if this goes on someone else will have to go short and get none at all. I know of one or two cases where owners of ordinary small suburban gardens have bought three and even four ounces, just to be on the right side. This is not economy, this is greed, and at the present time it is extremely unpatriotic. You can get half a ton of onions from an ounce of seed if all the seeds grow to maturity and are properly cultivated. You don't want half a ton. A couple of hundredweight is enough for the average family, and you ought to get them easily from an ounce of seed if you are anything of a gardener. To buy too much, therefore, is an extravagant waste and should be avoided, not only in the case of onion seeds, but all other seeds too. May I repeat that the best way to make the most of the onion seed is to get it sown under glass if you can, and plant out the seedlings in May. If you are not very expert at raising onions, I have reason to believe that you will be able to buy plenty of young ones in the spring from local nurseries all ready for planting out. We shall undoubtedly want more onions, but because there happens to be a temporary shortage now, there is no point in overstocking the garden or allotment with them at the expense of other and equally

168

Whenever any little thing goes wrong, have it put right immediately, however small it may be, then little troubles won't grow into big ones." On another occasion he found a few weeds and tufts of grass in the gravel between the houses, and he quietly suggested that if we were going in for grass we might as well keep a cow to graze it, and get some milk. I made sure he didn't find any more weeds or broken glass. But how sound his advice was, and what a lot of troubles we could avoid if we never allowed them to accumulate. And how quickly they do accumulate in a garden. A dead or broken branch on a fruit tree, a sucker, or a few weeds, a rotten post, a broken latch on the gate or a hole in the fence. We pass such things several times a day, and they would only take a few minutes to put right, but it is so easy to put them off, and they never get done. All the well-known pests and diseases of the garden could be prevented by taking timely measures, but we usually wait till they reach serious proportions, then it takes a lot more time and costs a lot more to deal with them. Surely one of the best forms of economy is to observe the old saying, "Never put off till to-morrow what you can do to-day," and never allow troubles to accumulate. How nice it is to go into the garden of a tidy-minded, methodical man. I have one or two friends like that; never a weed to be seen or anything out of place, sticks and sundries neatly stacked and the shed as smart and tidy as a drawing-room, so that no matter what they want they know exactly where to put their hand on it, even in the dark, and they never seem to be in a hurry, or to get behind with their work. I wish to goodness I could be like that. I usually have to move half the stuff in my shed to find the thing I want, and always forget where I left it, and usually find that I've lent it to somebody and can't remember who. We could avoid irritation and some valuable time if we could only cultivate those tidy, methodical habits, and the work would be much easier.

I was talking to a doctor friend of mine one day who had just completed an hour or two's work, and was putting his tools away. First he brushed his spade with a stiff brush, then rubbed it well with a rough cloth till it shone like silver, then he finished by rubbing it over with an oily rag. It took him only a few minutes, and he was chatting all the time. Finally, he took it to the shed and hung it in its proper place in a rack with the other tools, and I'm willing to bet a penny that you couldn't have found a speck of dirt on any of them; they might almost have been a set of surgical instruments. I believe it would have worried him if they had been otherwise. Contrast this with the man who, when he finishes his digging, scrapes his boots on his spade, then bangs it against the trunk of the apple tree and leaves it there, or puts it in a corner with half an inch of dirt plastered all over it, and as rusty as old scrap iron. Which do you think does the best work, and gets the most pleasure out of it? Which represents true economy? We could make our work much easier and more enjoyable if we only paid more attention to these simple little details. But I'm afraid if I carry on any longer in this strain I shall be accused of preaching at you. I am often being accused of saying something or other which I didn't really mean. I'm afraid I expressed myself badly when talking about gardening as a career for girls. I am told I was over-gloomy about the prospects; perhaps I was! The last thing I want to do is to turn any girl against such a career if she has a leaning that way, and really has her heart in it. Many girls have done remarkably well at it, and after a period at one of the horticultural colleges have taken the National Diploma in Horticulture, the highest qualification in practical gardening, and have blossomed forth as Government Inspectors, County Instructresses, or have secured good positions in the commercial world. These girls were sticklers and not afraid to work, and as I said before, there are plenty of girls to-day who can tackle any job and do it as well as a man. But I frequently meet another type of girl, who doesn't like dirty fingers, and who seems to think of garden work as a pleasant round of gathering flowers, or attending to them in a greenhouse or a shop, and I try to warn these girls that professional gardening is not just a rosy picnic, to be undertaken because they are delicate and unfit for other work; it means work and study, and a good deal of grit and determination. If I put the case badly and said anything to discourage the fine type of girls who are likely to make a success of a gardening career, and there are many such, then I am sorry.

Last week I spoke of the need for keeping small front gardens bright and cheerful. This brings a letter from a suburban dweller who points out that he has a corner house on a modern estate, and that his garden is on three sides of the house and almost entirely in full view of passers by. He is particularly keen on growing vegetables, but doesn't want his garden to be an eyesore in a smartly kept road, what can I suggest to combine utility with beauty. Now why should a vegetable garden be an eyesore? I hope I have never suggested anything like that. A well-kept vegetable garden can be almost as beautiful, and quite as interesting, as a flower garden, and I am prepared to say that if he stocks his corner garden entirely with vegetables and keeps it smart and tidy, it will create as much interest among passers-by as any of the flower gardens, perhaps more at the present time. Vegetables are full of beauty and interest to those who look for it. Take the main path from the gate to the front door. What about a border each side of it of, say, beetroots and carrots, designed in beds or groups, with an edging of parsley or chives, or perhaps thyme or other herbs. A group or two of sweet corn as dot plants, or a few single plants of curly kale, which are as handsome as a fern. Perhaps a group of red cabbages which are not unlike a rose in appearance, if you use your imagination a little. The border could be backed by a row of runner beans, which surely has a beauty of its own, especially when the scarlet flowers are at their best. A nicely staked row of peas is always good to look at, and could be planted like the beans, to form a dividing fence or a background. So could a row of Jerusalem artichokes, which stand up stately and green and make an excellent screen. Personally I like to see a well-cropped vegetable garden, and I can't think of any vegetable which has no beauty at all, except perhaps a batch of badly blighted potatoes or caterpillar-eaten cabbages, and there is no excuse for them. I saw some allotments last summer which looked good enough to be photographed or painted and used as Christmas cards. I wish I had thought of it at the time, I could

173

have sent out "Dig for Victory" Christmas cards, which would have been most appropriate. As it was I didn't send any at all, for which lapse I ask forgiveness from all concerned. But please don't think of vegetables as ugly or uninteresting, they are not. They are as attractive as they are useful, and worthy of pride of place even in the most conspicuous garden.

SOLDIER GARDENERS

I HAVE been asked to talk to you for a few minutes a out the soldiers' garden, or the camp allotment, or whatever you like to call it. I daresay, at first sight, the idea of doing a bit of gardening, and growing vegetables, is not particularly attractive to a soldier, especially if he has never been garden minded before, but, believe me, you can find quite a lot of pleasure and interest in gardening, if you set about it properly. There's a big difference between digging a garden and digging trenches, especially when there are plenty of you to take turns at it. It's like everything else in the army, the first month is the worst, after that you begin to enjoy it. Of course you may get a move on, and leave the results of your work for somebody else to enjoy, or on the other hand, you might enjoy the fruits of somebody else's labour. It's all in the day's work, so tackle it with a cheerful spirit, and remember that every extra pound of grub you can produce from the ground in the camp or outpost, is that much more towards the national effort, and that much less to be carted about, and there's nothing like fresh vegetables to keep you fit.

Of course I know that some of you who may be listening to me are old hands at the game, and are already good peace-time gardeners, so you must forgive me if I am rather elementary and start at the beginning, because I am going to assume that most of you know little or nothing about it. Perhaps some of you don't want to, but you can take it from me that if you are fond of a bit of outdoor exercise there is no more satisfying hobby in the world than an allotment. It's profitable and it is interesting, because you can watch your work develop, and the ever-changing crops are constantly providing new experiences and interests. It keeps you in touch with others like yourself: there is a kind of freemasonry among the gardening fraternity, they like to get together and talk over their experiences and exchange ideas. A kind of friendly rivalry and the spirit of competition is encouraged, and when, as a result of your labours, you cut your first marrow or cauliflower, you will get quite a kick out of it.

But before you can get results there is work to be done, so let me assume that you are starting at the beginning and taking over a piece of vacant ground. It may be land which has already been cultivated, if so you are lucky. On the other hand, it may be part of a grass field, or waste ground covered with weeds and rubbish. In either case, the first job is to tackle the spade work. You must dig, and dig deep. It has been said that the soil is full of treasure if you like to dig for it, and this, in a sense, is true, for the more and the deeper you dig the more will your efforts be crowned with success. Nearly all our vegetables like to send their roots down into the depths in search of food and moisture, and they can't do that in a hard, stony or water-logged soil; deep digging lets the air into it and gives the roots more room to ramble about, and when the dry weather comes you soon see the difference between crops on well-dug ground and those on shallow ground. What do we mean exactly by deep digging? To put it in a nutshell it means this: you must thoroughly break up the soil, two spades deep, or as deep as you can, without bringing the lower soil to the top, or burying the top layer of soil down below. At the same time you bury, at least a spade's depth below the surface, all the grass, rubbish and leaves and any old stable manure or any waste vegetable matter you can get, anything in fact, except the roots of strong weeds, such as nettles, docks and dandelions, which must be picked out and burned.

Suppose you are breaking up a grass patch. Start by digging a trench across one end of the plot about two feet wide and a good spade's depth, and try to maintain that trench at its full width all through your digging. The art of good digging consists largely in keeping a good open trench. Next break up the bottom of the trench with a fork to loosen the subsoil, then skim off the next two feet or so of turf and put it grass down, at the bottom of the trench, chopping it up with the spade as you do so. If you are not digging grass land, put all the rubbish and leaves and stuff in the trench. Then proceed to turn over the next spit to the other side till your first trench is filled up and a second one has appeared. Then break up the bottom, and keep on repeating the process until the work is done. The soil you took from the first trench can be used to fill up the last one. Don't take too much at a spadeful, it only makes the work harder and less thorough, and don't break up the soil to try to leave a nice smooth surface; the rougher you leave it the better at this time of the year. It allows the frost to penetrate and do its useful work. In the spring, before planting or sowing, the surface can be forked over and raked down to produce a fine tilth, but not now. If the land is heavy and sticky and difficult to work, a dressing of lime will help; about twenty-eight pounds per square rod of finely ground or slaked lime spread over the surface. (You know what a square rod is, don't you? $30\frac{1}{4}$ square yards, or a square bit of land $5\frac{1}{2}$ yards each way.) It's a good plan, too, to spread over heavy soil all the ashes you can find, except coal ashes or cinders, which are not good. Chimney soot, flue dust, brick dust, or old builders' rubble are all good for a heavy soil, so are autumn leaves from the trees, they help to keep it open and porous. Light soil, on the other hand, likes plenty of rotten spongy stuff dug into it, such as old grass mowings, spent hops, peat moss litter or cow muck, anything which makes it more spongy and helps it to hold moisture in the dry weather.

That will have to do for the digging. Once you have got that off your mind you'll find the rest of it easy and interesting. The next job is to decide what you are going to grow and to make plans accordingly: a nice little job for a wet evening. The haphazard or careless gardener usually starts off in the spring by sowing a row of peas or parsnips, or whichever of the vegetables occurs to him, only to find later on that some of them are in the wrong place and are holding up the planting of his winter crops. The wise gardener, on the other hand, sits down with pencil and paper and works all this sort of thing out in advance, and when the spring comes, not only is the ground all ready, but he has a complete scheme of cropping, so that each of his vegetables fits naturally into its appointed place. We don't know how long this war business is going on, but I suppose we

178

ought to assume that the camps and gardens will last for a few more years, and plan accordingly: if they are not needed the year after next so much the better, but let us be on the safe side. One of the first things to consider in a cropping scheme is a system of rotation which will ensure that no crop occupies the same ground in two successive years. Different crops take different chemicals from the soil, and one may leave behind something which another one requires, so by changing the crops round regularly the soil does not become exhausted, but it soon would if you kept on growing the same kind of stuff on it year after year. There are several ways of cropping a piece of ground for rotation, and I daresay some of you could work out a good scheme for yourselves, but for the want of a better one I suggest that a simple way is to classify the crops according to their season of maturity. Start by dividing the ground into three equal sections. Put all your early crops on one, your second early or late summer crops on the second section, and your late or winter crops on the third. The next year you can change them round so that your early crops follow the late summer crops and they in turn follow the previous year's late crops. It works out quite easily, and avoids overcrowding and inter-cropping. Take the first section first: here you will sow early turnips, stump-rooted carrots, round beets, early dwarf peas, French beans, early potatoes, lettuces, broad beans and so on. These will be used up during the summer in time to clear the ground for brussels sprouts and other winter greens. On the second section you can put your mid-season potatoes, such as Majestic, King Edward and Great Scot, summer cabbages, peas and

179

anything which can be cleared in September, to give plenty of time for a bit of autumn digging. The third section is used for your root crops: parsnips, swedes, winter carrots, beets, runner beans and anything which has to occupy the ground till late in the autumn, and as you clear it during the winter the ground can be dug a bit at a time in readiness for the spring. That, of course, is a very brief way of putting it, but if you once get the idea you won't find it difficult to work out the details. While we are making plans let us consider which are the most important vegetables to grow; this is, of course, a matter of opinion or individual taste, but in war-time I think most of us are inclined towards those which give the heaviest returns for the least outlay and trouble. Presently you will be making out your seed list for next spring, and it is just as well to consider these points. One important point is to cater for all the year round, and spread over your crops so that there is always a fresh vegetable of some sort available. So many beginners have an abundance of stuff in August and September, but little or nothing in March and April, the months of scarcity. That is the result of bad planning and must be avoided. Some vegetables are in use all the year round, and they must be considered first: potatoes for instance. You are sure to want a pretty good supply of potatoes, and I suggest you should bank on mid-season varieties, such as Majestic and Great Scot, which crop heavily and can be lifted and stored in September, before blight and slugs play Old Harry with them. You'll want a few earlies, no doubt: the first new potatoes are a just reward for the gardener's industry, but, unless you've got a very large area of ground, you mustn't overdo them. A few rows of, say, Sharpe's Express or Eclipse, are as good as any. By the way, if you've grown a good crop of potatoes this year, why not make the most of them and stop all that wasteful peeling. I watched some troops recently peeling potatoes and they were throwing half of them, and the best half too, away. The greatest food value of a potato is just under the skin, and wherever possible they should be boiled in their skins and eaten whole, or just the outer skin peeled off after cooking. Two potatoes cooked in this way are equal to half a dozen peeled ones, and a much better flavour too! I think we ought to watch over the preparation and cooking of all the vegetables. There is a terrible lot of waste going on, which is not very encouraging to those who have worked hard to grow them. The next important crop is the onion, which is getting very scarce because the supply of imported onions has dried up. Good old onion, we hear a good many jokes about it, but it's the mainstay of many a tasty dish, and I'm afraid we shall miss it sadly if we can't get it. We ought to grow as many as ever we can next year.

We must choose the deepest and best ground for onions, because they like to be generously treated. Carrots, too, are always useful, and likely to be scarce. We can keep up the supply all the year round: little stump-rooted kinds during the summer and autumn, and long ones to store for the winter and spring. Beetroots, parsnips and garden swedes are useful vegetables for the winter, and quite easy to grow. A nice row or two of runner beans are always welcome, and they will grow almost anywhere. The dwarf French beans are an excellent crop to grow for harvesting for use during the winter instead of imported haricots, so we ought to include a goodly supply of them. Of course we mustn't forget the greenstuff. By a little manœuvring we can have a green vegetable every week in the year. Round summer spinach, New Zealand spinach, and spinach beet will keep up the supply nearly all the year round. The spring cabbages you have already planted will turn in for May and June; then a few cauliflowers, and the beans and things will see us through till the autumn, when the brussels sprouts begin, and after them the savoys, to be followed in the early spring by the kales and purple-sprouting broccoli, which will see us through till the spring cabbages come round again. Another vegetable we mustn't overlook is the leek, one of the most useful of all, because you can get it when there is precious little else to be had. It is all a question of planning in advance, and all I am trying to do now is to put ideas into your heads to help you in drawing up your plans. Perhaps we shall have an opportunity later on of discussing the details of sowing and cultivation. Meanwhile, I hope you will all have a look at the little leaflet, "Notes on the Autumn Programme in the Vegetable Garden." It's a War Office publication of 5th October. However, here are one or two final hints.

When planning, give everything plenty of room, you gain nothing by overcrowding. Get rid of all rubbish, it only breeds disease; and never put away your tools in a dirty condition. Oil them and clean them and make as much fuss of them as you do of your rifle.

Set about the job with a big heart. Learn all you can

from the failures and successes of others: and although you may get an occasional disappointment, you will soon become interested and, I hope, enthusiastic, and find that the oldest occupation on earth is still one of the finest and most profitable forms of recreation.

GETTING TOGETHER

To-DAY I want to talk to those of you who are living in the comparative peace and security of country villages. I have visited a great many villages lately and I have received the impression that the desire to help the common cause, the enthusiasm and the spirit of national service, is as keen and strong as in the towns. So far the testing times, the nights of misery and anxiety, have not reached the villages to the same extent, and so the opportunity for national service is not as great as many would like it, indeed, in some remote villages the war still seems a long way off, and more than once I have heard people say they would like to do war work of some kind if there was anything useful that they *could* do. Well, there is! There is the Dig for Victory campaign; the production of food, not a very spectacular undertaking, perhaps, no uniform or glory attached to it, but as vital and as patriotic a job as any which is being tackled. Please don't misunderstand me, I don't suggest for a moment that the villages are not digging for victory. I know that they are, very extensively, and I should think very few villages have had to buy vegetables from outside during the past season. But I want to go a step further and see the villages not only feeding themselves but producing a substantial surplus to help feed the towns-people who have no opportunity of growing anything for themselves.

With a little organisation it could easily be done. In the early days of the war, when we were pushing the Grow More Food campaign, we were rather too fond

184

of saying that the idea was for each gardener or allotment holder to grow enough to feed his own family but not to grow it for sale. I'm not sure that we were right there, in fact I'm quite sure we were wrong. The idea was right enough in urban districts where space is restricted, and where, if a man can grow enough for his own needs, and thus save transport, he is doing useful national service, but in country villages, with their spacious gardens, this always has been done. Therefore, if the present war effort only aims at doing what we always have done, just supplying ourselves, there isn't much in it. On the other hand, the average villager, having grown enough vegetables for the needs of his family, has little or no inducement to grow more, because he wouldn't know what to do with it if he did. He could hardly be expected, even if he had the time, to push a barrow load of cabbages or something several miles to the town to make a few coppers profit out of them. This is the weak spot in the scheme which must be put right. There is still any amount of vacant ground in villages, which could and should be producing food for the towns. The country villages could add thousands of tons of food to the national supply and do themselves a bit of good at the same time. Suppose, for example, a small country village this year had produced an extra ton of onions—say one hundredweight each by twenty allotment holders or cottagers; that wouldn't have meant much extra labour, but they could easily have sold them in the wholesale market for £50, and suppose a thousand villages did the same or double the amount, work it out yourselves and see what it would mean: extra money coming into the villages, extra food for the towns, and it could be done as easily as shelling peas, but how?

Well, I think the first thing to do is to form a local gardening society on co-operative lines. Some villages have one already. Most of the towns and urban districts have one, but the majority of villages have not, and many of those which did exist have petered out because the annual flower show had to be dropped. I should like to see a war-time association formed in every village in the country. There is usually someone who has a little spare time and could set the ball rolling. What I suggest is that a public meeting should be called of all those interested in gardening. A show of hands would soon indicate whether people wanted to form an association. That point decided, the next thing is to elect the team of officers and get down to business. In a small village which I have been associated with, we recently started such an association, and I have been astonished at the support and enthusiasm which has been forthcoming; it seemed as though the men had been eagerly looking for the opportunity to do something of the kind, and have grasped it with both hands. The new secretary, a very live wire, immediately got into touch with the County Council, the Royal Horti-cultural Society and other official bodies, and collected all the information likely to be of use to him; a set of rules was drawn up, and an annual subscription of a shilling for membership was agreed on. Already we have over sixty members. That may not sound much to you but it represents nearly all the able-bodied men in the village. Fourteen additional allotment plots have been taken, nearly four tons of seed potatoes and over two tons of lime and fertilisers have already been ordered at very low rates, so that in this deal alone many of the members have more than recovered the shilling subscription. As time goes on more and more supplies will be bought in bulk at the special low prices made possible by the County Council and the Ministry of Agriculture. Under these official schemes, and by the co-operation of the large seed firms, local associations can buy the best of everything they need, often at not much more than half the usual prices, which is, of course, a tremendous advantage. Well, I think you'll agree that that isn't a bad start. Now what of the future possibilities? I am going to make a few suggestions to those who are willing to make a similar effort. First, you must be careful in the choice of officers; the secretary, for instance, need not necessarily be a good gardener, although if he is, so much the better, but he or she should be a man or woman of tact, with good organising and administrative ability, one who is respected and able to lead. A good secretary makes all the difference in the world to the success of an association, so for that matter do the other officers, such as the chairman and the committee. They should be chosen for their ability, and not on personal grounds. Too often, in villages, we get square pegs in round holes. We also get far too much petty jealousy, and a sprinkling of cantankerous people who adopt a "shan't play" attitude if they can't get their own way in everything. All that sort of childishness must be dropped in war-time, and we must all work together.

Having settled this point, the secretary should get in touch with the Horticultural Superintendent of his

County Council, who will give him a great deal of useful information as to official schemes for advice and assistance and tell him about the National Allotments Society and the advantages of affiliation, and so on. The Royal Horticultural Society, Westminster, will also help. Among other things, the society publishes a useful leaflet showing how to form a new association, draw up rules, and so on. Once the secretary is armed with this sort of information, he will see his way much more clearly as to future procedure.

Having made a start, and got the new association safely launched, the next thing to do is to keep the members together and prevent apathy or dry rot setting in after the first wave of enthusiasm has evaporated a little. I can only make vague suggestions here, to be adapted to local circumstances, but I am a great believer in giving a social flavour to a gardening association, which might otherwise get a bit dry and uninteresting. I suggest that if at all possible, a regular monthly meeting should be arranged, so that the members could gather together, and arrange for a member to give a short paper on a garden subject, to be followed by a general discussion, or an outsider could be invited now and then to give a lecture. Members should always be encouraged to talk, not expected to sit quietly in rows like children at Sunday School, while one does all the talking. Make it free and easy, so that members can discuss their problems and experiences. Another good plan is to encourage members to bring small exhibits to the monthly meeting, not only vegetables, but perhaps a bunch of sweet peas or other flowers, a dish of fruit, or even a freak of some kind. Such things create interest, and provide a basis for discussion. If desired, a programme could be drawn up, making one particular vegetable the subject for each evening, according to season; points could be awarded for the exhibits of, say, half a dozen leeks, beetroots, onions or potatoes, as the case might be, the points to accumulate throughout the year, culminating in a championship prize for the highest score. The vegetables would be taken home again and there would be no waste. There are quite a number of possible variations of this idea. An annual show in the Village Hall, followed by a whist drive and dance, might be a nice way of rounding off the season's work.

Now I am coming to what I consider the most important part of the business: the disposal of surplus. If my experience is any guide, I should say that every member of such an association could quite easily produce a hundredweight of vegetables over and above the family requirements; some of them, of course, could produce a great deal more. In the small village I have in mind that would mean two and a half tons, and it is that two and a half tons which ought to find its way into the towns where it may be urgently needed. I suggest that at one of the winter meetings the association should decide on certain vegetables to be grown by the members for marketing, and if I were asked to decide that point I should say the non-perishable vegetables which can be used during the winter, and are more convenient to handle. Onions and carrots would be my first choice. If I am anything of a prophet I should say that onions and carrots will be in short supply for a long time to come. In normal times we spend at least £2,000,000 a year on imported onions, and at

G   189

less than a penny a pound you get a deuce of a lot
of onions for £2,000,000, far more than we are likely
to grow ourselves; but if every village in the country
could supply a ton for general consumption it would
be a very real help, and they would get more than a
penny a pound for them too.

Very well, if every member grew his quota of
whatever was decided on, the whole could be collected
together in due season after the harvest, arrangements
could be made for delivery to the wholesaler in the
market, and the proceeds shared back among the
members; they would get the cash and the towns would
get the food, which should prove a mutually agreeable
arrangement. I see no great difficulty about it, the
demand is there and likely to be for a long time; it is
up to those who can to see about the supply, and
certainly the country villages can do a lot towards it,
if they will only organise and work together; it can't
be done individually.

Already, in many districts, arrangements are in
existence for the collection and sale of surplus produce.
The Women's Institutes are doing a good deal in that
direction, and groups of them often have their own
stall in the market town, where they dispose of a great
deal of surplus produce, an excellent piece of work too,
and I see no reason why the local horticultural society
should not co-operate with the Women's Institutes,
and sell their surplus perishable vegetables all through
the season in addition to the special crops already
mentioned.

As I said before, I am only throwing out vague
suggestions, local conditions have to be taken into

consideration and arrangements made accordingly. But let us make the effort and do what we can. Remember that it is work of real national importance; every onion, carrot or potato sent by the villages to the towns is almost as helpful as the bullet or shell sent by the factories to the fighting forces. Therefore I appeal to the villages to organise themselves for more and more food production, and to make a start now.

C. H. MIDDLETON AND F. H. GRISEWOOD

Middleton.—It seems a long time, and a great deal has happened, since we had our old friend Mr. Grisewood with us in these talks, so I am particularly happy to welcome him back again. I'm afraid his experiences this time are rather on the sorry side, for his beloved country garden, which, you will remember, was at one time growing in beauty day by day, has had to be abandoned, and Mr. Grisewood no longer wields the spade with the cheerful vim and vigour he once did. How's that for an introduction, Freddie?

Grisewood.—Not bad! At least it has the merit of being true. My war-time duties have kept me constantly in Town, and I'm afraid all my well-laid schemes for digging and sowing and reaping have had to go by the board, at least for the time being. I see very little of the country now, but I'm just as keen as ever, and before long I hope to stir up the weeds a bit, and then we'll soon make up for lost time.

M.—We surely will, and while we are looking forward what are we going to talk about; what schemes have you got for the future?

G.—Very vague ones at present, I'm afraid, except that instead of talking about lilac and roses and rockeries, we must now turn our attention more to the kitchen. Now, you know vegetable growing has never been my strong point, so I shall be glad of a few tips, ready for the spring. Early peas and potatoes to begin with. Tell me how to get them really early.

M.—Well, there are always ways and means of doing

it, but for my part I think the craze for earliness is often overdone. Sometimes in a favourable spring, by sowing or planting early on a sheltered border you may gain a week or two, but as often as not you gain nothing. There is always a bit of a gamble about it, and I often think I would rather wait a bit and be on the safe side, especially in war-time.

G.—I daresay, but it may not be war-time when I get going again. In any case, I don't want to lose anything by reckless gambling, but you must admit that after a long weary winter, with the daily "taters" and greens and parsnips, those first early peas and new potatoes are delightful, they make you lift up your heart and rejoice, and anything which can do that in these dreary days is worth striving for. I've sometimes been to friends at Easter time and had delicious new potatoes, and I've said to myself, if they can get them, why can't I?

M.—You can, if you've got the necessary glass accommodation; but you won't get them at Easter out of doors, you'll be lucky if you get a decent spring cabbage by that time. But if you possess a small greenhouse, or a few garden frames you can get quite a lot of things early. A good many people do possess these things but, to my mind, don't make full use of them; they could add considerably to the food supply in these times, and as you say provide a few of the luxuries which make life worth living.

G.—That's just my point. I don't want to gamble with early crops at the expense of the normal supplies, but if we can get something early in addition to the ordinary crops, surely it's worth while?

M.—I quite agree.

G.—How do you grow new potatoes under glass?

M.—Provided you've got a greenhouse with a little warmth in it, you can grow them in large pots or boxes, two or three tubers in each, according to size. You must choose a first early variety such as May Queen, and put them about five inches deep. Plant them in late January and stand the pots where they get all the light possible, and when they begin to grow you must give them fresh air too. Give them water when necessary, but not too much, and gradually more ventilation as they grow, until the lower leaves begin to turn yellow; then you turn them out of the pots and sort them over and if you're lucky you'll find some nice tender little potatoes, but don't expect the pot to be packed with them because it won't be. Meanwhile, if you've got a cold frame or two, you can make up a bed of soil in one of them and plant some in the middle of February, about nine inches apart; these will follow the pot crop, but you must look out for frost, and cover the lights with straw or mats to protect them on cold nights. On the other hand, once they are growing well, you must take the lights off altogether in mild weather, they must have ventilation.

G.—When would they be ready to dig?

M.—Early in May, with ordinary luck.

G.—Good, now what about peas?

M.—They are not so easy. I think your best plan with them would be to sow some in a frame in early February, gradually harden them off as they grow, and plant them out on a sheltered border early in March. You should select one of the early dwarf varieties with round, smooth seeds, not wrinkled seeds, and if you've got plenty of little pots, put one seed in a pot, the same as you do with the sweet peas; they transplant better that way. Some people sow them in autumn, but it's a bit too late for that now. Dwarf French beans are a better crop for the greenhouse. If you choose an early variety such as Superlative, or Ne Plus Ultra, and sow them in January in pots or deep boxes, with the seeds three inches apart, you can often get a nice early crop. But you mustn't coddle them. They must be kept cool, and get plenty of fresh air and light.

G.—If you've got a warm greenhouse doing nothing why not start now?

M.—You don't gain anything by it. Warmth alone isn't enough. If you try to hurry things by keeping them warm you defeat your own object. Daylight is most important. There is very little growth during the declining days of December. Once the turn comes and the days begin to lengthen, Nature responds to the call, but not before. You must always remember that in forcing vegetables you are merely advancing the season for them. Normally they grow out of doors in the spring and summer, and under glass you try to reproduce as nearly as possible the spring and summer temperatures and conditions; it's no use exaggerating it and creating tropical conditions, especially for the hardier kinds, they just won't have it.

G.—Yes, I can see that point. Now what about sweet little spring carrots?

M.—The garden frame is the best place for them. Make up a bed of soil and start sowing them in early February, protect them from the hard weather and give them fresh air when possible. Sow them thinly and then don't disturb them till the biggest are ready. You can also grow early snowball turnips and radishes in the frame. You can raise early lettuces and onions for planting out in the spring. It's a long story, but anyone with a little ingenuity can get all sorts of early and extra crops by making full use of a row of garden frames.

G.—That's the sort of thing I should rather like to do. Now to jump from the sublime to the possibly ridiculous, what about the man who can only spare very limited time, at fairly long intervals. What are the easiest crops for him? How many of the farm crops would be worth growing on an allotment?

M.—It depends what you mean by farm crops and where you draw the line. You could grow most of them in a garden, but it doesn't follow that you would like to eat them.

G.—Well, take swedes for instance. They are good wholesome food for the winter, as everybody knows. I've never tasted mangel-wurzels cooked, have you?

M.—I'm not sure what you're getting at; if I say yes, you'll probably say something about being appropriate, but as a matter of fact, I have.

G.—What do they taste like?

M.—Something rather like sour beetroot.

G.—That doesn't sound too good. What about field or horse beans? There must be good food value in them, couldn't they take the place of haricots in war-time? You could easily grow a few bushels of them.

M.—You might get frisky and start kicking if you ate too many of them.

G.—That's just what I should like.

196

M.—I've eaten them when they are young in the summer and shelled them like peas. They are quite good then, rather like little broad beans. I don't know what they would be like in the winter, I expect they would want a lot of soaking and cooking, and the skins might be a bit tough. I must try them and see.

G.—Perhaps some of our listeners have already tried and might give us their opinion.

M.—Yes! Of course we are already growing the dwarf French beans for drying for winter use. They are quite good. I would just as soon have them as imported haricots. Do you like beans?

G.—Yes, I like broad beans when they are very young, but not when they get old and leathery and you get them served up covered with foul-tasting white sauce.

M.—Some people say the best way to eat broad beans is to eat them very young, pods and all, like runners.

G.—I tried that once, but I wasn't impressed, perhaps they were a bit too old, and they were rather like boiled flannel. Talking about pods, you mentioned sugar peas once, what do they taste like?

M.—Excellent. I consider them an ideal war-time vegetable. There is a variety called Paramount, grows about six feet high and produces a tremendous crop. I've had pods seven inches long and full of good peas, but the pods themselves are thick and fleshy, and instead of shelling them you could eat pod and all and they just melt in your mouth. They are very sweet and don't need sugar with them which is another advantage. They are economical too, half a dozen pods goes as far as a couple of dozen when they are shelled.

G.—Don't the pods get stringy?

M.—They may do a bit when they get old, but you can let them get full size before there is any sign of it, particularly this variety Paramount, which I had last summer. What do you call your favourite vegetable?

G.—I don't know that I have one; I like most of them. All vegetables are nice if they are properly cooked, and they can all be nasty if they're not. I like peas and asparagus.

M.—No doubt, but you were getting down to swedes and horse beans and mangel-wurzels just now, what about striking a medium?

G.—Very well, spinach. I'm very fond of spinach, but I always had difficulty in getting good leaves on it, it started flowering too quickly. I suppose that was due to my light soil. How can you keep up a supply of spinach over the longest period?

M.—You must grow the different types to do that. Start in March by sowing a couple of rows of the true or summer spinach. The secret of that is a rich moist soil, and a sheltered, semi-shaded situation. In the summer, especially in a sunny dry situation, it starts flowering, as you say, too quickly, but if you sow it in the shade, and water it, it does much better; but it's usually a bit difficult after midsummer. A better plan is to sow a bed of New Zealand spinach to follow the other in the late summer.

G.—That's the cut and come again kind, isn't it?

M.—Yes, you keep picking the shoots and leaves off the same plants.

G.—I've often been going to try it, but never have, it's easy enough, isn't it?

M.—Yes, you can sow it in a frame in small pots

198

in March, one seed in a pot, and plant it out in May, or you can sow it out of doors in May. You know how to grow nasturtiums! Well if you give New Zealand spinach exactly the same treatment you won't be far wrong. It spreads about just like a nasturtium plant, so you must give each plant about two feet of space. It lasts well into the autumn and to follow that you can sow a row or two of spinach beet. That is really a kind of beetroot, but you keep picking off the other leaves, and if you sow them in the summer they will often keep growing right through the winter. You can also sow a row or two in September of the prickly seeded spinach, that comes in very useful in the winter, too.

G.—And do they all have the same sort of flavour?

M.—More or less, if you use your imagination a little. The spinach beet is a rather stronger flavour. Some people prefer the New Zealand type, but personally I don't think any of them are quite up to the ordinary summer spinach, if you cut it fresh and tender. But they are all acceptable.

G.—What about salads, one of my difficulties has always been to keep up a constant supply. I think there is nothing nicer on earth than a good salad. I would have it every day if I could, but when the lettuces and tomatoes are over it isn't easy.

M.—Perhaps you stick too much to the orthodox things, there are plenty of salads besides lettuces and tomatoes. You can have endive well into the winter, by growing the plants like lettuces in the late summer, and then covering them with plates or mats or something to turn them white, a few at a time, about three weeks before you want them. You can grow cos lettuce in rows like spinach in the autumn or early spring, or in boxes in the greenhouse like mustard and cress and cut it young. You can shred up the heart of a cabbage, you can force old beetroots, carrots or swedes, or dandelions, in a warm dark place, and the young tops are quite good as salad. You can use nasturtium leaves, you can grow land cress and lambs lettuce. All these and a good many others can be worked into a mixed salad. I have even had apples shredded up with the other ingredients and never noticed them. And of course there are always spring onions and chives, and odd leaves from some of the herbs which all add to the flavour of a salad; some people grate up raw carrots in it. I always maintain that any average gardener should be able to produce a salad if you are not too fussy what it is, and you make a nice dressing for it.

G.—Ah, there's the rub; it's something like Sam Weller with the meat pies, it's the seasoning or, in this case, the dressing, what does it.

M.—Round off.